BRIGHTEN
YOUR
LEADERSHIP
LIGHT

GARY HASSENSTAB

ISBN 978-1-0980-7739-6 (paperback)
ISBN 978-1-0980-7740-2 (digital)

Christian Faith Publishing, Inc.
832 Park Avenue
Meadville, PA 16335
www.christianfaithpublishing.com

Printed in the United States of America

CONTENTS

PREFACE

Each of us as humans and as members of a society, community, and/or organization bring a presence or "light" to the other members of that group. It's kind of like you pretty much always have your personality on display for all to see. As long as you are breathing, you have a personality of some type. A personality goes with the territory of being an interactive social entity. As a leader of a team, your presence or personality, because of the impact it has on the lives of others, is your part of your leadership "light." As a leader, you are expected to light the way with your leadership skills, behaviors, and values that you emanate to your organization. When you break it all down, your teams and your organizations are expecting those with leadership roles, formal or informal, to show the way for people to achieve and sustain success so the organization can also be successful. You have a leadership light. You cannot choose not to have one. Just like you cannot choose to have a personality. Fundamentally, your only choices are how bright you want your light to be and asking yourself if you are shining your leadership light in the right direction to achieve organizational success. This book will help you gather the skills, behaviors, and values to first assess the brightness and quality of your leadership light. In addition, the exercises provided, when performed with sincerity and truth, will help you brighten your light to more clearly "show the way" for those you are leading.

Lightbulbs are measured by wattage and lumens. Wattage being the energy used by the bulb to the complete its one and only task: to produce light. Lumens are the measure of the quantity of visible light, i.e., degree of brightness produced by the bulb. Leaders have a light as well, sort of a leadership luminescence. That brightness and clarity of your values, future vision, tactical direction, and actions directly impact your organization's success. So for a leader, your actions display your leadership brightness. Your values, style, words, and behaviors are then the factors that determine your leadership lumens—your visible leadership light, i.e., the brightness. The same way that the voltage, type of light bulb, electrical power delivered to the light socket, clarity of the glass of the bulb, etc., influence the output of the bulb, your output is formed by all the things a leader brings every day to their role and interactions with their teams. Unfortunately, there is no way to label a leader with a leadership version of "lumens." However, everyone the leader interacts with has already internalized a lumens-like value based on their own observations. So if everyone else has pretty much given you a leadership lumens score, you should probably assess yourself and determine the brightness (or dimness) of your leadership presence, and then be active in the growth of your leadership light to others.

BRIGHTEN YOUR LEADERSHIP LIGHT: CREATE THE HABITS FOR YOUR GROWTH

You are the light of the world. A city that is set on a hill cannot be hidden. Nor do they light a lamp and put it under a basket, but on a lampstand, and it gives light to all who are in the house. Let your light so shine before men, that they may see your good works and glorify your Father in heaven.
—Matthew 5:14–16

We are what we repeatedly do. Excellence then, is not an act, but a habit.
—Aristotle

The energy and power of "habits" create the brightness. The clarity of your "values" aims your leadership light. Both are essential sources of energy and brightness for your leadership light. This book is to help you build habits around two basic leadership competencies that I think are foundational to all other leadership skills—skills that result ultimately in a set of behaviors that drive a leader's actions and determines the brightness and effectiveness of your leadership. It is through your actions, or inactions, that then influence the culture. It is your actions which then drives the behaviors and actions of the people needed to actually accomplish (or not) tasks which further (or not) the mission and vision of the organization and brighten your light. Those two leadership habits and competencies are self-awareness and effective communication in order to perpetuate the needed and desired set of values to drive organizational success. Values drive behaviors. Behaviors drive actions or inactions. Actions or inactions will drive, or deter, results. Results achieve success or failure. Hence, the value of "values" and the power of habits.

No one should care more than you about your development and growth of leadership skills based on positive values. No one will care more, except of course, for the team of people who are looking to you, depending on you, hungry for you, to become a great leader and wonderful manager who will create a great environment for them to all succeed and do things that make them proud. People want to come to work at a place that aligns with their values, provides good work to accomplish good things, and be treated with respect. Those are basic ingredients to creating employees who are engaged in their teams and company's success and are generally glad to be employed by the company and reporting to you. It is critical that leaders have an embedded habit to examine their own performance that is impacting the team's success. Meaning, to make it a habit to examine their own actions or inactions, determine if that was a good or bad behavior, and if that behavior is driven by the right and positive set of personal values.

Self-awareness creates the ability to change, grow, adapt, and absorb the inevitable changes to your organization and what it takes for you and your team to be successful. Self-awareness (knowledge) is foundational to effective self-management (actions). Strong knowledge and propensity to take action is key to evolving you to be a more effective leader. Evolving your skills and approach to what is needed will have a higher degree of success if you truly understand your current skills, values, weaknesses, and leadership style. An increase in our self-awareness will come at a cost. As you upgrade your self-awareness, you will be degrading pretty much the exact opposite skill: self-deception. Self-deception is really just our ability to successfully lie to ourselves. Most of us get pretty good at that ability. The results of self-deception are generally that we feel better about ourselves, and who doesn't like that! So we grow this ability, which at least in the moment makes us happy and it usually becomes quite ingrained in our habits. This makes the work to increase self-awareness even more challenging. Self-awareness then is the ability to be truthful and honest, and view ourselves, our actions, motives, etc. through the lens of reality and not the prism of our wishes.

Self-deception on display in a management/leadership role usually shows up as a form or variation of "I'm the manager, so I am always right." Self-deception can often incorrectly equate title to degree of perfection. Therefore, the higher the manager is in the organization chart, the more perfect they are. Comical thinking to be sure. However, more subtly, self-deception can cause a leader to become rigid and blind to the need to recognize that they need change, adapt, and grow themselves and their leadership behaviors. They then develop blind spots to the needs of their teams to stay or become more effective and their own role in evolving their teams to higher levels of capabilities and contribution. As the people and teams grow or decline, the organization grows or declines in its capability to remain successful.

The exercises in this book will also connect your growing self-awareness to the consequences, good or bad, within your organization. I use playing poker as an analogy to strong self-awareness. If you have played poker or any kind of cards with a group of people on a regular basis, odds are they have discovered your "tells," meaning little things you do differently based on the cards you have been dealt, and they know when you really have a good hand versus when you are bluffing. Therefore, the smarter (i.e., more self-aware) you are of your "tells," the more you can control or use them to be more effective at playing poker. Your "tells" are often emotion-based actions. Building the skills and habits that increase your self-awareness is tied to your ability to perceive and examine the emotions driving your words and actions. This is nothing new. John D. Mayer, PhD, a psychology professor at the University of New Hampshire, and Peter Salovey, a professor of social psychology and president of Yale University, researched and wrote about the concept of emotional intelligence relative to management effectiveness three decades ago.

Daniel Goleman's work and writings on *Emotional Intelligence* are a great source of a more in-depth perspective on this topic. Goleman popularized with the idea that being a genius with a really high IQ and being the most skilled in the technical aspects of the role or job would not create a well-rounded and truly effective organizational leader. Self-awareness as an aspect of emotional intelligence is a key factor toward success. Goleman's contributions are great source to better understand the role self-awareness plays in your success and growth. I highly recommend becoming quite familiar with his publications.

Effective communication creates the values and culture needed for the organization to be effective. There is tremendous value in *proactively* defining "values" through your communications in words and deeds. Values in an organization exist, whether or not a leader declares them as so. Values are like the air we breathe. Values are the atmosphere that is created and then influences the organization. Values generate and then influence the culture. To get us on the same page on culture, I will insert here one the classic definition of organizational culture as "the underlying beliefs, assumptions, values and ways of interacting that contribute to the unique social and psychological environment of an organization." A more common definition is "it's the way we do things around here." Culture rules, like it or not, effective or not, warts and all.

The "atmosphere" in the organization will exist, whether or not we name the values that generate the atmosphere. The organizational culture, as an output of the collective values, stated and unstated, is really making many of the decisions taking place in an organization. People are just a delivery mechanism for a culture-induced action. Culture and organizational values often determine which stakeholder's needs get priority and win out and which stakeholders get the short end of the stick. Culture can also facilitate progress and correct ineffective decision-making and actions taken by leaders. However, it is more often a hindrance if the culture is "fixed" quite firmly to reinforce the status quo and can sabotage the evolution that organizations need to undertake to stay relevant in their market space. Our actions as leaders support and reinforce or modify this atmosphere, whether or not we had that intention. The atmosphere and the humans within it react. Similar to Newton's third law of physics, for every action, there is a reaction. We cannot always precisely choose the reaction we will get to our action. We as leaders must observe and learn from ourselves and how our actions influence or cause reactions within the atmosphere and are demonstrated in the culture. A leader will either taint or enrich the organizational atmosphere often with the most subtle actions or words.

Part of this book will be guiding leaders to name their values. It is important to actually name or label the target of our actions. Naming something helps make it come alive and seem more real and tangible to us. Leaders need to be conscious, aware, and active at naming, choosing, and enabling the values they want guiding their organizations. The values needed to generate the atmosphere and then the culture will then unleash the engagement and value their people can provide to drive the prosperity of that organization.

You will see that throughout the chapters, I will interject quotes relative to the topic being presented. I have found over the course of learning more about how to be an effective leader that focuses on creating highly engaged teams that produce great results for the organization, that quotes from people much smarter than me help me focus and simplify a concept to a short couple of sentences. I use quotes from the great leaders over the decades or even centuries to help crystalize the concept into a few sentences or words.

You will see that throughout the chapters, I will interject quotes from the Old or New Testament of the Bible relative to the topic being presented. Now I do not claim to be a great biblical scholar or even a mediocre one. However, over the years I have read some (but not nearly all) various chapters of the Bible for my own spiritual growth. Proverbs, Wisdoms, the four Gospels, Acts of the Apostles, and the various New Testament letters are those books that most resonated with me. I always seem to come away with some type of connection from a story or quote relevant to this day and age. For this book I sought out quotes that I felt provided guidance or context to the topic at hand. Regardless of where you might be on your own spiritual journey, I wanted to connect these concepts to an idea or belief to some basic Christian tenets about our purpose here on earth. Perhaps your leadership role is really part of God's plan for how He wants to use you to make a difference in this world. As a disclaimer, as stated above, no one will ever confuse me as an expert on the Bible. Also, I am not espousing any specific Christian religion over any other. In reality, during the course of my work on this book, I found it interesting that other non-Christian religions had similar types of philosophies as those I used from the Bible. Perhaps some concepts about treating people with honesty and respect and helping others succeed and produce good fruits of their labors crosses religious boundaries.

I relate the relationship between the leadership research that has been done over the decades, meaning the "science" of leadership, with the wisdoms from the teachings of the Bible with this quote from Dr. Martin Luther King Jr:

> *Science investigates; religion interprets. Science gives man knowledge, which is power; religion gives man wisdom, which is control. Science deals mainly with facts; religion deals mainly with values. The two are not rivals.*

The tools to increase self-awareness and to define and instigate the values you want to build will be simple. Taking pen to paper will be the old-fashioned, old-school method to build this set of skills and habits. From adult learning practices, the more senses that a person involves in the learning activity, the stronger the neural connections that get created in the brain, then better retention and understanding is created. There is value in that kinesthetic connection of the brain to the hand to the pen and back to the brain created by the reflection exercises.

I recommend that for the reflection questions you will see at the end of each chapter, you do the following:

1. Read it. Duh! Visual learning is step 1.
2. Read it again—out loud. So now you hear the words spoken, plus your brain had to connect to your speech centers

and send the words to your mouth. Auditory learning is step 2.

3. Underline a key word or two in the question. You have now brought in the physical senses in to the understanding process. You have now used several muscles! That's the next level of learning.

4. Ponder a bit, mull it over in your head. Relax, give it some time to sink in.

5. Talk to yourself. Tell yourself out loud your answer. Also just a tip: don't do this part on the bus ride to or from work. You may get some odd looks from the other passengers.

6. Write down your answer in the book or another journal if you choose. Pen or pencil to paper.

7. Reread your answer out loud. Does it sound reasonable? Coach yourself; tell yourself, "Nice job."

These steps will complete a cycle of bringing in visual, auditory, and kinesthetic learning to both the comprehension of the question and then the development and creation of your answer. The steps above are the first part of the learning process—self-examination of your actions and behaviors. In addition, you need to approach your learning from a position of humility—accepting that your perspective and skills are incomplete. Then have a sense of curiosity and a beginner's mindset to really explore the concepts and exercises presented here. However, always recognize you are smart and doing good work. Some of the reflections may elicit answers from yourself that may bum you out. Don't let it. We all have limitations and flaws. None of these exercises are meant to erode your self-esteem. In fact, congratulate yourself that you had the courage to be honest with yourself, and then be just a little more proud of yourself.

Hopefully you will take this self-reflection to the next level and create what I call an "aha" moment. Meaning you pondered at a deeper level and thought about the ramifications, potential or real, of your actions on your team, organization, family, or even yourself. That deeper level can then come alive. The "aha" light bulb goes off in your head. You might hear your brain saying to you, "Oh, so that is why the team got really quiet in the team meeting. It was because I had really dismissed their suggestions as weak, without even exploring the pros and cons of each." Now reinforce this "aha" learning and this capability with a few simple steps:

1. First of all, write down your "aha" statement in full. Perhaps even expand with additional examples or outcomes that connect the action or behavior on which you reflected. As you can see, I am a believer that if something is important, *write it down*.

2. Put your "aha" into a headline. A short phrase or sentence, ten words or less, that captures the essence of your learning. Perhaps for the example above, the headline might be: *"Quick judgmental responses killed team engagement."*

3. Now greater understanding and increased self-awareness alone will not guarantee you will become a better leader. You must add in *actions* to generate change and create new habits and behaviors. No surprise there—right? There is a difference between knowing something and actually doing something. The knowledge and understanding alone that you need to eat less and exercise more to achieve a healthy weight will be of little value without a defined action plan to diet and exercise that you can track and hold yourself accountable for. This is where your self-management comes into play, or the lack of self-management will hold you back. The final step is to create an action item and, of course, write it down. I recommend your action items not just be purely the actions you will take. Provide the context for the action by framing it within a problem statement. Therefore, you begin your action items declaration with a problem statement to communicate back to you "why" you are choosing to assign yourself this action and how you will track and hold yourself accountable.

    Example: *My routine or natural style has been that I immediately see and express the reasons why an idea from the team will not work.* My behavior *is shutting down engagement from the team. In the future I will have a reminder to myself before my team meetings to first ask inquiring questions as my initial response. Responses such as "That sounds really interesting, what do the rest of you think?" or "Let's first examine the list of positive outcomes on using that idea. Then, let's stress test it and see what gaps it might have."*

4. A method to work on this action item is to ask yourself an open-ended question beginning with the words "*How might I...*" This will open up your thinking to an internal brainstorming. You will come up with suggestions and give yourself options. To continue with the example, "How might I respond in a manner that would generate more engaged thinking from the team?"

You will see a page for each chapter to serve as a parking lot for all the headlines and action plans created in their own sections. First, let us do a practice round on at this type of introspection. Here is your first exercise.

Within the scope of your work life, the role you are fulfilling, and the organization you are in, what are the *values* that you want to be known for by your team? By your manager? By your customer (meaning the person or organization that really depends on you and your team to deliver something of value)?

If you could only build your reputation on three values, what would those be?

1. _____

2. _____

3. _____

Why did you select these three?

1. _____

2. _____

3. _____

How do you *know* you display these values on a daily basis?

1. _____

2. _____

3. _____

How should you better display the key values on a daily basis?

1. _____

2. _____

3. _____

The chapters to follow will present a set of values that, first of all, are critical to building and leading successful organizations. Secondly, like all values and habits, they can only grow and flourish in leaders who have developed a competency around self-awareness and effective communication skills. Now, do I think these values are the absolute final and complete set of values for leaders? Nope—I am not nearly that wise! I have included a list of wonderful and much wiser authors and books to help you continue to learn and grow later in this book. However, I think these are a good foundational set of values that when second nature to a leader, will elevate the level of performance in their organizations.

When the righteous are in authority,
the people rejoice, But when a wicked
man rules, people groan.
—Proverbs 29:2

When your values are clear to you, making
decisions becomes easier. (Roy E. Disney)

Value this book will focus on:

1. *Integrity and honesty*—Nothing that positive will ever happen without a leader acting consistently and genuinely in a way that generates trusted and engaged followers.
2. *People-focused*—Leaders are humans leading other humans to deliver organizational success. People, not "resources," are the deliverers of results.
3. *Results-focused*—And speaking of results, a leader and their teams are expected to actually do something useful and needed by the organization.
4. *Do the right thing, the right priorities*—The tug-of-war for your attention and focus can often lead you astray from a focus on what is really important.
5. *Deliver great value to others*—An objective for a leader is to help others be more effective. Be of service to all that you can.
6. *Appreciate and value your teams*—This is to show others you value them, especially those for whom you rely on to deliver the results needed.
7. *Communicate with respect*—One of the foundational leadership values that seems to be a struggle.
8. *Unlock the potential of your team and organization*—Your leadership stewardship demands that you elevate the skills and engagement of your team and your organization.
9. *Unlock your potential;* continue to learn—You matter and so does your growth as a person.

10. *Keep a healthy perspective;* balance family, faith, and career—
   An important personal value to have is to realize life is not
   only about a paycheck.

Now on to the next chapter and the beginning of your learning journey.

> *Let nothing be done through selfish ambition*
> *or conceit, but in lowliness of mind let*
> *each esteem others better than himself.*
> —Philippians 2:3

> *Above all, it is necessary for a person to have*
> *a true self-estimate, for we commonly think*
> *we can do more than we really can.*
> —Seneca, first-century philosopher

CHAPTER 1

EMANATE INTEGRITY AND HONESTY

*He who walks with integrity walks securely, but
he who perverts his ways will become known.*
—Proverbs 10:9

*The supreme quality for leadership is
unquestionably integrity. Without it, no real success
is possible, no matter whether it is on a section
gang, a football field, in an army, or in an office.*
—Dwight D. Eisenhower

Yeah I know, the concept of including honesty and integrity in a
leadership book is real original, right? Some leadership values have
pretty much endured over the generations. Honesty and integrity are
two behaviors that cross generations, cultures, and in any industry.
Why? Well, there are just some basic elements of human nature and
of the dynamics of a group of people formed into an entity called a
team that endure as well. People are still people, with the same basic
thinking processes, fears, survival instincts, and quirks that make
us unique as when Frederick Taylor defined the human elements of
organizational life in his findings on organizational behaviors. The
"organization" still has its own personality that interacts and influences the human players that coexist within it. So this chapter exists
because honesty and integrity still matter.

Leaders, managers, team members, and people in general all have their own triggers that cause them, often unconsciously, to act with various degrees of dishonesty and act in ways that depart from the words they speak. Therefore, their actions and words do not align, i.e., a lack of integrity. People, *including you*, are flawed and will fall short of perfection often. Robert Greenleaf in *Servant Leadership* wrote about the "half people" we all are because we are all incomplete and a work in progress. We will all fall short sometimes in the areas of honesty and integrity. So let's cover this topic first to work on your self-awareness in this area.

Honestly is more than telling the truth or not telling the truth. It is not binary. It can be fuzzy because "things," like your words and actions, get judged by the brains of the observers of that event. Therefore, it will pass through multiple layers and variations of people's paradigms, life experiences, and perceptions of the actors involved in the "event." The perception of honesty, or an action to be honest or dishonest, to some degree is influenced by the receiver or observer of the action and their perception of the degree of honesty of the person whose action is being observed. Simply put, people do "consider the source" when interpreting and judging the actions and words of others. That judgment is just part of basic human nature. It is akin to a survival skill wired into our brains. Our brains are wired to seek the truth we need for our survival. Knowing whom we can believe and trust is often very much an issue of survival in the workplace. Perhaps not always physical survival, but this survival instinct can be just as much about protecting ourselves from mental, emotional, and *career* injury as well.

Honesty and integrity are not for the faint of heart. Whether you like it or not, your actions, behaviors, reactions, inactions, words, nonverbals, whatever, are being assessed and judged by everyone based on their brains, not yours. This judgment by others impacts the quality and brightness of your leadership in their eyes. And you can't change that with just your *words*. For example, saying you are going to exercise will not burn any of that annoying belly fat. It takes actions that align with your words. You can only control you. So that is why this is the initial chapter. You will need to be courageous, possibly even painfully so at times. Therefore, you need to initially get really good at self-awareness, relative to how honest you even think you are being. In addition, learning how well integrated and how well-aligned your actions are to your values, and hopefully the values you want to propagate in your team and organization, is a definition of integrity. Integrity can be viewed, in my opinion as, does everything I do, send the same message as to what I value and consider true and "right." Are you always speaking and acting to do what is right? Which does not mean "being right." It is the age-old statement of "doing what is right." Note: it is "doing" and not just "saying" what is right.

Integrity is your words backed up by your actions. Your integrity and how it is perceived is the first element of your style that will filter or possibly dim your leadership light. It is important for you to have that awareness, that it is the *perception* of your integrity that others have of you that matters. Your actions and words, through the course of all the interactions, influences the perceptions of others, whether you like it or not. In addition, no one is that good of an actor that they can maintain a facade of solid honesty and integrity over time. No one.

Now time for some fun. Replay that past month, week, day, whatever in your head. Rerun your last team meeting. Review your last customer meeting. Think about the last hallway conversation you had with someone.

Review the decisions you've made or actions you took during the day or week and write down the values communicated in those decisions. *Were those the right values?* The values that correctly represent you *as the person and leader you want to be?* The values you prioritized back in the previous chapter?

———————————————————————————————

———————————————————————————————

———————————————————————————————

Where did your words and actions conflict with each other and shade your leadership light?

_____

_____

_____

By the way, the smart money would bet because we are flawed, that at some point misalignment between your words and your actions did take place at some point in the past week. A good place to look is to review the most "pressured" decision or action you took. Pressure, stress, friction, conflict—all those nasty big and little events that pop up will have tendency to hijack our rational and normally values-based thinking processes. This can cause our neurons to misconnect and cause our brains to make choices that are at odds with our values. The end result being that we choose which problem to live with and therefore act with less than true honesty and integrity to the right values. Keep in mind that "less than true honesty" does not mean you are necessarily blatantly lying. This often comes out as not being completely candid and honest—so not giving false information, just not giving all the information or feedback. Often we will justify this choice by choosing to be compassionate toward the receiver of our actions. You may choose to hold back on feedback because it may hurt someone's feelings or be discouraging to a team and impact morale. So first of all, congratulate yourself for being a leader with an empathetic gene in your DNA. I commend you for taking the few seconds to ponder how others might react. You then effectively make a choice based on a set of values. One of your values might be to be considerate of others. Or another value might be to treat information with the degree of confidentiality that is needed. So not telling someone or a team something based on other relevant and overriding values may be quite acceptable. Making the choice to do the right thing is often being comfortable with shades of gray between multiple values.

So just between you and yourself, how honest have you been with yourself, your team, your customer, your manager? How authentic have you been with the people above?

A truism you should memorize is that everyone has an "antenna" that can detect disingenuous actions—meaning, people can detect, to some degree, when someone is not being honest and not displaying integrity to them. Crudely put, we all have a "BS meter." So the old saying "You can fool some of the people some of the time…" is probably less true in this era of increasing skepticism of those in authority in society in general. It would be wise to assume that approaching your team with a facade of honesty and integrity will only work for a few people and have a short shelf life. So thinking you can fake honesty is probably a bad plan.

Hey, it's easy to be honest when things are going well and according to plan and your desires. However, your genuine values, honesty, and integrity will be tested when "things" hit the fan, so to speak. Pressure, conflict, and bad news all get our brains back into survival mode and our true values and selves can become visible. You may have to make tough decisions and trade-offs between values that are important to you. A strong sense of self-awareness can still guide you to keep alignment and integrity between your words and your actions when the pressure is on. Or you can think you can fake it until the storm passes. Good luck. However, you are really gambling with your effectiveness as a leader by choosing a path that deviates from integrity and honesty. So just between you and yourself, do you think you are really that good of an actor?

Pray for us; for we are confident that
we have a good conscience, in all
things desiring to live honorably.
—Hebrews 13:18

What situations challenge you to maintain your honesty and integrity? What was the trigger in the situation that caused you not to perform up to your expectations?

_____

_____

_____

What would you like to do differently based on what you discovered during this chapter? List possible action items below. How might you create more integrity between your words and actions? How might you create just a bit of space between the event and the decision you need to make, so, you can really think it through and truly determine the values to be considered before taking an action or making a decision? *Think, then act.*

_____

_____

_____

Who in the organization do you trust and why?

_____

_____

_____

Why would people genuinely trust you? Note: Do NOT SKIP THIS QUESTION. Trust is such a fundamental leadership characteristic that you genuinely need to develop your self-awareness on your actions and behaviors that increase or decrease the level of trust in your organization.

_____

_____

_____

What is your headline for what you learned about yourself, your behaviors, intents, actions, etc.? What was the "aha" from this section? Fill in the section below with ten words or less.

_____

_____

_____

Now, this may be the most important instruction of each chapter. If you could do *one thing* differently, and hopefully, better and more effective next week to align with (i.e., have integrity with) the values you desire to communicate and the values of the organization, what would it be? Just one thing that you want to do differently and supremely well. Be courageous. Write it down.

_____

_____

_____

_____

What you just did above was only the initial step. Now, write down how you are going to remind yourself and hold yourself accountable to the "one thing" you just defined.

_____

_____

_____

> *Let me be weighed on honest scales,*
> *that God may know my integrity.*
> —Job 31:6

> *No legacy is a rich as honesty.*
> —William Shakespeare

CHAPTER 2

BE PEOPLE FOCUSED

*Let nothing be done through selfish ambition
or conceit, but in lowliness of mind let each
esteem others better than himself. Let each of
you look out not only for his own interests,
but also for the interests of others.*
—Philippians 2:3–4

*If your actions inspire others to dream more, learn
more, do more and become more, you are a leader.*
—John Quincy Adams

Unless robotic process automation has defined your team as a squad of bots, I will assume that you actually interact with teams of real humans. Therefore, odds are pretty good you actually need other humans to leverage their brain power, experience, specific skills, and knowledge, and *willingness*, to deliver all the above to the benefit of the organizational mission and goals. This chapter will cover the topic of how to get the best from the people you lead. Hopefully, these humans actually look to you for direction, assignments, short- and long-term goals, and respect you to the degree that they will give their best effort to achieve these goals, follow your direction, or simply solve the problems that reared up today. People "show up" for work in varying degrees. The first level is physically showing up, relatively on time and when expected. However, showing up (or not) *mentally and emotionally* can be difficult to determine. The person's mental and emotional "presence" really drives the value that a manager and their organization receives from that person.

An effective leader needs to understand what they are doing, or need to do, to impact a person's mental and emotional presence to engage the team's *collective* brainpower and willingness to actively produce great results. An effective leader needs to fully grasp that the directive that their stewardship to the organization and to the people they lead is to get *their team* to do great things for the organization. Remember, your leadership light is intended to be seen by others, perceived as a good thing, and then followed by the people in your organization. "Followed" being the key verb. Whether you choose it or not, just by your role, your leadership style and values are essentially like a guiding light or star that people will follow to some degree until you give them a reason not to.

Fortunately, there has been gobs of good research on the topic of employee engagement and motivation over the past several decades. The concept of "engagement" is generally thought to have first come to be defined and measured with employee survey work done by the Gallup organization back in the 1990s. The book *First, Break all the Rules* by Gallup analysts Buckingham and Coffman used the Gallup data to define the characteristics of a strong and positive workplace. Gallup eventually developed a survey product specifically to measure employee engagement. To summarize the variety of engagement definitions out there, I think engagement can be boiled down to these factors. First, it is a state of mind. That "state" generates a mental and *emotional* perspective related to the person's work environment. The environment includes the job and tasks, coworkers, management relationships, reward systems, customer interaction, and the physical world. Most of the items mentioned in the previous sentence (rewards, nice office, safe conditions, and good people) are what Frederick Herzberg defined as hygiene factors that lead to satisfaction or dissatisfaction with the job. People physically show up when they are satisfied and will engage the necessary parts of their intellect and skills to get the job done. However, the engagement level, which is influenced by their treatment and relationship with their leader, creates the emotional and mental perspective to deliver passion and caring about doing great work and contributing to team and organizational success. The result is the degree of energy, passion, ownership, and creative thinking brought to the job by the person.

I like a definition of engagement from Wilmar Schaufeli who defined it as a "positive, fulfilling, work-related state of mind characterized by vigor, dedication, and absorption." Therefore, it is how a person "feels" and how that drives their physical behaviors that gets work done. This can often be summed up as "attitude." Therefore, employee engagement may not seem rational, at least to you. But the summation of all the job factors from the perspective of the employee's brain causes that person to make both conscious and unconscious choices on how they will approach, respond, and interact with the events that take place during the workday. The Gallup research has shown that "engagement" is a reliable predictor of employee performance, more so than a measurement of employee "satisfaction." As their leader and manager, you can, *and do*, influence attitude and engagement, but you cannot control it to suit your needs. You are in charge but not in control. Repeat that line to yourself each morning.

I am betting you have been exposed to a variety of engagement/motivation theories and philosophies in your own training. I found Abraham Maslow's hierarchy of needs as a useful guide or template to guide a leader in understanding the nature of employee motivation and engagement. There are likely other models as well, but again being old school, I like the simplicity of the theory Z model. For the most part, the job probably provides for the physical needs, meaning, a paycheck that helps the person put food on the table. Also in general, for a business environment, the need for "safety" level 2 is also accomplished without the manager doing a heck of a lot. But satisfying the higher needs, like belonging to a community of people, being recognized as a valued human being, and then doing things that drives a sense of pride and fulfillment, can be overlooked because they can be kind of that "touchy feely" aspect of management.

However, generating an environment or "atmosphere" that creates the sense that people enjoy and feel safe within the team, there is mutual respect and an interdependency with others where people complement strengths and mitigate each other's weaknesses. Leaders need to assess their impact on that atmosphere and if the levels of mutual respect, safety, and interdependence are where they need to be for success. To start with, people need to understand how and why they, as people with their skills and their contributions, are valued by the organization. People perform better when they feel their efforts and output has meaning and value to someone. This is not a new idea. This common sense approach to understanding the fundamentals of employee motivation is not a brand-new discovery. However, this truism of motivations seems to be an area that leaders often overlook. My experience is that people are promoted into management roles, in part, because they were really smart, skilled, and proficient at completing the tasks and objectives of their nonmanagement role. Therefore, the culture created a value and rewarded "task completion." Except now as a manager, your job is to get task completion through the efforts of others, meaning, your team. The focus often goes right to delivering the end results—a completed task instead of a focus on creating highly skilled and effective people and teams to deliver the completed tasks and results.

The better approach and your primary objective as a leader is to create that atmosphere of high team engagement to release the energy and potential of your team. Your job is to unleash the tremendous brainpower and creativity of the people in the team *and* get their heart and energy into high gear to generate great work and value for the organization. Your job is to evolve the team into a community of leadership that then elevates the leadership capacity of the entire organization—which, in the end, will come back to you and set you up to be viewed as the great manager and leader that you are because you increased the leadership capacity of the entire organization.

Let's start off with some basics that a leader should know about their team. You will see there are a lot of topics to address and questions to answer. Read through them all first. Then decide which set seems most interesting or perhaps most uncomfortable to you and address those first. You can always come back and focus on the remaining ones.

> *True leadership must be for the benefit of*
> *the followers, not to enrich the leader.*
> —John C. Maxwell

Every leader should know the following: Who are your stars? Why?

_____

_____

_____

Why do they stay with you or the company? What are your stars passionate about in their jobs? What gets them excited about coming to work? What challenges them? What do they find rewarding? Do you really know?

_____

_____

_____

_____

_____

Why would they leave? What causes them to lose motivation and passion for their jobs? What drives your stars nuts or frustrates them?

_____

_____

_____

Who will be your stars in three years? Do they know you feel that way about them?

_____

_____

_____

For your entire team, by person, list the most important *one* skill or capability that they need to grow in over the two to three years to be more effective, more successful, and provide more value.

_____

_____

_____

Unless you are the manager of a prison work program, all your employees are really volunteers. Expressing gratitude to your truly "volunteer" workforce is a core leadership skill and behavior and always will be. To whom and how have you said thanks this week? If the answer is "no one," are you really sure that no one did anything good for you to show some level of gratitude? If you really want to blow someone's mind and make an impression, actually say thank you with a real thank you note. I know, how old-school, right? No one does thank you cards anymore. Be special. Stand out from the crowd. Use a simple thank you card and write a few words as to what they did and why you appreciated it and put it in their work area. Maybe even go crazy and put a little smiley face on it. A simple gesture delivered with style and panache that delivers a powerful message. If you want to create more impact, put a stamp on it and mail it them. You remember stamps, right? *So whom have you thanked in the past month?*

_____

_____

_____

By the way, how do you remind yourself to say "thanks" to people? If the answer is "I don't," then that just might be an action item for you for this chapter because odds are you do not say thanks enough.

_____

_____

_____

In the past week, to whom did you make the effort to seek out to talk to? Whom have you not talked to and why?

_____

_____

_____

What is the best thing the team accomplished this past week? Whom in your team have you recognized to the leadership level above you?

_____

_____

_____

What are the top three habits you need the people in your organization to have to be highly effective? Notice, I asked about "habits" and not skills. Do they know how you would answer this?

_____

_____

_____

How well are they doing at these habits? How do you know?

_____

_____

_____

Who is most in need of your guidance to grow in their role and career? Who seems to be struggling?

_____

_____

_____

BRIGHTEN YOUR LEADERSHIP LIGHT

Before you are leader, success is all about
growing yourself. When you become a leader,
success is all about growing others.
                                        —Jack Welch

Considering Jack Welch's advice, here are a couple more challenging questions which may stretch your ability to be honest with yourself.

Why is your team better because you are their manager?

_____

_____

_____

How would your team answer this question: "I would go work for (you) anywhere, anytime because

_____."

How would they answer this question: "I would *not* go work for (you) if I had a choice because

_____."

Don't accept your dog's admiration as
conclusive evidence that you are wonderful.
                                        —Ann Landers

Just a side note, surveys have shown that about a third of employees would be relieved if their manager moved on to another role or even company. So if the above question was easy to answer and you needed more than one line to answer, you might be in that group of managers that your team would prefer not to work for, so own up to that. Say no to your self-deception and embrace that you now have a targeted area to improve.

What is your ten-word headline for this chapter on your performance as a people-focused leader? What was the "aha" from this section?

_____

_____

_____

What would like to do differently based on what you discovered during this chapter? List possible action items below.

_____

_____

_____

As in the previous chapter, just pick one thing from the list above that you would like to start with, and do supremely well, to brighten your light to your organization. Now, write down that first thing and how you are going to remind yourself and hold yourself accountable to being successful.

_____

_____

_____

But Moses' hands became heavy; so they took a stone and put it under him, and he sat on it. And Aaron and Hur supported his hands, one on one side, and the other on the other side; and his hands were steady until the going down of the sun.
—Exodus 17:12

You can design and create, and build the most wonderful place in the world. But it takes people to make the dream a reality.
—Walt Disney

CHAPTER 3

DRIVE FOR RESULTS

He shall be like a tree planted by the rivers
of water, that brings forth its fruit in its
season, whose leaf also shall not wither;
And whatever he does shall prosper.
—Psalm 1:3

Concentrate on the few things that will produce
the greatest results. Force yourself to set priorities.
Do first things first—and second things not at all.
—Peter F. Drucker

Lest you think this journal is just an exercise to be a great "people" manager, this chapter is about why your team or organization exists, and why you are in your leadership role. Your primary purpose, objective *numero uno*, is most likely to get something good and valuable done for the organization that helps the organization and everyone in it prosper. Your role and your team exists for a reason: *to get great results*. Not just to do hard work, but to actually deliver great results from that hard work. I will assume you are able to communicate the reason for the team's existence from, not only your perspective, but from the view of those above you as well. Something to consider is that your team will likely have an understanding and perspective of what they define as results and success. Odds are pretty good that the team's view of the results they need to deliver are actually not too far off from what the organization defines as success. Will those two views align 100 percent? Probably not. However, it is probably in the same ballpark.

Hopefully, the team will have a personal and team view of the results being delivered by the team. However, it is a problem if each person and then the team as a unit does not really know how to discern the results they are producing and whether those results are good or not. Moreover, it is your problem as their leader. I have mentioned that what a leader truly values is reflected in what they ask and talk about. The opposite is also true. From a team member's view, if my manager never asks me how my work is progressing, then what I am producing must not be all that important or valued to him/her or the organization.

However, most team members will have a "personalized" view of the results they are striving to achieve. Your team members will have desired results unique to them that speak to their own objectives for career goals, family goals, relationships, acceptable stress, etc. that combine to define their view of success. People, being the selfish (just kidding) but rational humans that they are, will likely have stated and unstated desires of the results they want to achieve. They likely will also want to be part of a successful team and organization. Therefore, people will want to contribute to the team's success and be considered "being part of a thriving community," i.e., Maslow's levels.

You can also view the team as a "person" that can be examined with the same Maslow levels from his theory Z on employee motivation. Your team is made up of rational human beings who want to be successful and achieve things that make them proud. A first cousin, perhaps, of Maslow model is Clayton Alderfer's ERG model that condenses Maslow's levels into three basic needs of people/teams. The base need is to remain in *existence* and have access to all the basic building blocks of a sustainable life (food, water, shelter, etc.). The next level is a person's need to *relate*, meaning, to other humans in some relationship or sense of community. The third level is *growth*, which is the human need to accomplish something, become better, more skilled, and humans who are realizing their potential (the self-actualization of Maslow's hierarchy). You will see that a common thread or theme throughout most models on engagement is that people do want to have opportunities to achieve something of value. They want to produce results that mean something good to someone else.

Your objective as a leader is to keep everyone's eyes on the prize. Your leadership light needs to foster a team environment that maintains high visibility and focus on all the various short- and long-term objectives, all the tasks that need to be completed, all the fires that need fighting, and all problems that need to be solved. Illuminate the results that need to be produced. In addition, you need to uncover all the issues that are eroding the team's ability to generate the results needed for the team and organization to succeed. James Autry, in his book *For Love and Profit*, referred to this responsibility as a leader's role in "creating the place" where people come together and are able to do great work. At the end of the day, the team has got to get something of value done and delivered. You need to enable the team to do great work because that is your job. You can attack that objective from two opposite ends. The easiest, perhaps, is to determine what you as the leader need to add to the environment—the tools, capabilities, skills, capacities, processes, recognition, etc. that are enablers to the team to get great work completed. However, you can and should also view it from the other end: what do you need to remove from the tools, tasks, processes, etc. that actually are a drag on the team's capabilities to produce? There is "addition by subtraction" by eliminating no-value tasks or time wasters. Looking for areas to eliminate no or low value activities will be part of the learning exercises for this chapter.

Your team really wants to be successful. So make it easy and clear for them to know what "success" looks like to you and the organization. It is important to put a spotlight on and make it clear how you intend to track, manage, and follow up on the output delivered by the team you are leading. Then actually perform the follow-up actions you described to the team because it is a safe bet that if you do not ask about or follow up to determine progress on results, any focus by the team on those results will wither away. Remember that chapter 1 presented how integrity is alignment between your words and your actions. Therefore, defining the results the team needs to produce and how you will measure progress are really just words. Certainly, those words are helpful and absolutely necessary; however, without tracking and follow up to show the team how successful they are toward the needed results, the words will quickly become more "empty" words from a manager.

Become a friendly "pest" to your team because the results they produce are so important to the organization and you also want your team to be successful and viewed as such by the rest of the organization. Show the team's progress, ask about their progress. Then ask what is working well and what is not and how you can help. Celebrate great results. Help the team correct and improve on mediocre progress. The key is to ask and talk about the important results needed early and often, i.e., be the friendly pest. Focus on outcomes.

However, a word of caution about being a friendly pest and not evolving into a micromanager because it can be a fine line between the two. Becoming a micromanager will come into play in the chapter on empowering your team. Meaning that being a micromanager will prevent any level of effective and true empowerment from becoming a mainstay of the culture in your team or organization. The pest I am referring to is a part of you that focuses on a few key words in the previous paragraph. You should see words like "success", "progress," "results," and "ask," As a results-oriented "pest" you are best served, at least initially, by being in inquiry mode and not tell/dictator mode.

There certainly is a time and a place that leaders may have to switch gears to get into full-blown "tell" mode. However, be careful so an autocratic style does not become a habit. Long term, that "tell" style will not create a truly engaged team. Actually, a consistent leadership style that is highly controlling will devolve a team from any level of engaged critical thinking. The organization will no longer offer new ideas because their leader does not listen anyway. Next, the team will reduce the amount of feedback given, initiative being shown, and ownership taken in results, and so on. In reality the only development activities they will undertake are those skills and experiences that get will them another job. However, there is a bright side to all this devolution by the team. Team meetings will be a whole lot shorter because no one, except the leader, is really saying much! Hey, if my opinion does not matter, then why bother offering it up? That is a sad state for a team to be in.

It is more effective long term for a leader to define the results needed by when and let the smart people that comprise your team determine how best to achieve those results. The "how" they achieve the results may not be exactly how you would do it, but often that may be just fine. I am not saying that the ends always justify the means. It is not quite a binary yes or no answer. You as a leader need to assess holistically on how the team performed relative to the target results and how the team achieved or missed on the targets. The team may have found a better way to get the results needed—because you did not dictate the "how." When that happens, the leadership light of you and the entire team is now a little bit brighter. Recognize and appreciate the intelligence, creativity, and engagement in the team. Engaged employees in collaborative team environments not only unleashes the potential of your teams, but that connection to the organization is a significant factor to reducing employee turnover. Desired results are the objective for any organization, but so is creating the culture that keeps the great people who produce those results for today and for the future. You won't go far without great people on the team.

Let us begin this chapter's exercises with some questions that should be top of mind for you and easy to capture.

What does a great job look like for your team? How would your team know that? Are you sure they do know?

_____

_____

_____

Why does the great job you defined above really matter? Why are those results relevant and to whom (and you do not count)? The "whom" is ideally a true customer of the organization's products or services or internal customers who need your team's output to be successful themselves.

_____

_____

_____

What do you expect your people to do and/or not do? Are your expectations a mystery to them? Have you ever asked if they knew your expectations? If your answer to the previous question is no, you could have some fun and ask them in a team meeting or one-on-ones to list five things you expect of them.

_____

_____

_____

What are the "numbers" you *and* the team use *to tell the truth* about how the team is performing? What are the metrics *and* the targets for each metric that are a scoreboard for results and accountability?

_____

_____

_____

Are these metrics visible to all the stakeholders? Do these metrics clearly show what victory looks like?

_____

_____

_____

Who or what do you worry about the most in your team's ability to get the results needed?

_____

_____

_____

Of the worries you listed above, which ones can you control or mitigate? And how will you do that?

_____

_____

_____

Now, let us look for opportunities to make the team more effective, perhaps more focused, and therefore more productive. What meetings or activities were a waste of time? By the way, odds are pretty good that most meetings are a waste for all or some of the attendees unless someone is bringing doughnuts. I have found that throughout time, certain meetings become "fixed" in the environment or culture, kind of like that ugly or broken chair in the conference room that no one wants to throw away. All "regular" meetings should have an end-of-life date that causes them to be reexamined every so often to determine if the event still has the right objectives (or any objective, for that matter) that actually provides value to the attendees.

In terms of the results they need to produce, what does your team do really well?

_____

_____

_____

To deliver to the objectives of the organization, in what three areas does your team need to improve?

_____

_____

_____

What can you can do to help your team produce even better results?

_____

_____

_____

A strong results focus can be summarized as Peter Drucker stated, "Put the first things first." As a leader, it is key to get you initially, and then your team, to saying yes and spending time on what really matters most for organizational success. Consider subordinating or maybe even ignoring, if you can, those demands on yourself and your team that do not matter. Below are some questions that focus more on stopping doing things that consume time on matters of less or maybe even no importance. "Addition through subtraction"—more than just a cliché!

What was the most useless meeting your team attended last week? How could their time have been better spent?

Is your team producing anything that no one consumes and likely never will or things that do not really matter or matter less in the grand scheme of things?

What environment do you want to create for the people who should be following your direction? Do your communications, in all forms, support the environment you want to create to get the results the organization needs?

What is your ten-word headline for your "aha" from this chapter on your performance as a results-focused leader?

_____

_____

_____

As in the previous chapter, pick one thing from the lists above that you would like to start with and do supremely well to generate great results from your team. Now write down that first thing and how you are going to remind yourself and hold yourself accountable to being successful.

_____

_____

_____

Meditate on these things; give yourself entirely to
them, that your progress may be evident to all.
—1 Timothy 4:15

Effective leadership is not about making
speeches or being liked; leadership is
defined by results not attributes.
—Peter Drucker

CHAPTER 4

DO THE RIGHT THING

And let us not grow weary while doing good, for in due season we shall reap if we do not lose heart.
—Galatians 6:9

Efficiency is doing things right.
Effectiveness is doing the right things.
—Peter F. Drucker

Rumor has it that we typically make thirty-five thousand decisions a day. Now like any internet "fact," that number may fall apart under scrutiny. But most likely we make a bunch, right? Most decisions may be somewhat trivial: which socks should I wear today? However, in the workplace most of your decisions will at some point be examined either in open conversation or in the recesses of people's thoughts. First, people are just examining your words to understand the decision. Then they will move quickly to what it means to them specifically. Next, they will be judging the decision based on whether the impact to them is good, bad, or neutral. However, somewhere in that analysis process, people are learning about what you consider important and a priority for the team to do, whether or not you intended that to be an outcome of your decision. Your decisions and actions shine your light on what is important.

A really effective leader does the right things at the right time. So what are the "right things"? This is where your organizational values, personal values, and ability to act with integrity often intersect.

Obviously there are some clear definitions of the right thing. Treating all people with respect. Following the ethical and principled actions of an honorable person. However, after that it may get cloudy when a manager has to decide between competing priorities for their time, attention, and for the support of their team. So for the purposes of this chapter, I am going to focus on the "right things" relative to your deliverables and especially the deliverables expected of the team. Odds are it is the norm in an organization that leaders and their teams have more demand for deliverables than they have capacity to deliver. That is often when "no win" decisions need to be made, which is what you get paid to do.

What are the most important "right things"? It depends, right? Organizational "right things" usually are communicated through vision statements, annual goals, projects, job guidelines, rules (written or not), and expectations (written or not). Also your expectations verbalized, written, overtly communicated or not, are really a form of principles guiding your team. In addition, often these items listed above and the current priorities will conflict with other "right" priorities. These conflicting priorities and goals then cause inconsistent expectations and therefore confusion and stress in the organization because you are asking your team to guess at which "right thing" might be at the top of the list this month or even today. Odds are pretty good people will guess wrong more often than correctly. Confusion and stress about what is right or a top priority are not ingredients that lead to highly engaged and productive teams.

Your priorities on all these goals, guidelines rules, projects, and expectations become evident through your actions, i.e., where you spend your time, your inactions, what you say and talk about, and what you do not say. Whether you choose it or not, your actions and behaviors, a.k.a. "leadership light," are revealing what you think are the most important priorities. As a leader, you owe it to your team and the organization to have integrity to the organizational "right things" in your words and actions. Therefore, this dilemma or paradox between competing or incongruent priorities is one of the challenges of your role that you need to develop the skills to handle effectively. Your team expects you to provide the clarity needed on what is important and a priority for them because, as stated before, they want to be successful and do what is right. Keep in mind that doing right may not always seem obvious to others, so don't make anyone guess or assume. Strong leaders create a clear and repeated message about what they stand for, how they operate, the culture they are trying to create within their teams, and what values they use to guide their actions.

Doing the right thing may not always be pleasant. Saying no to someone, giving tough feedback, or perhaps firing someone is not pleasant but may be the right thing to do. However, even the unpleasant actions you need to take do not need to make you an unpleasant person. You can do the painful "right things" in the right way. Organizations often face at some point actions, decisions, or strategies that may not be positively received but are needed for organizational health and continued progress. Even tough organization decisions might be the right thing to do, and you are part of the leadership team expected to carry out the plan. When it comes to the unpleasant communications that need to happen, cold and heartless may be efficient but is rarely the right thing to do. This is where organizational values come into play to help you make the right choices which by the way, you will not make 100 percent of the time. The organizational values and your personal values hopefully align pretty well on what are the "right things" for success. These values should ensure the focus of your light (i.e., leadership attention) is correctly shining on the truly most important right things, holistically, for the results needed and for the people under your stewardship.

Write down the top five to ten organizational "right things," i.e., important objectives, goals, priorities, or values that should guide you and your team. Which ones are "declared" priorities or values, meaning, they are written down somewhere? Which ones are implied and are really part of the organizational DNA and likely not written down? The unwritten priorities, rules, and guidelines in an organization are "gotchas" and should really come out from hiding and become apparent to your team.

_____

_____

_____

What are three things from the list above that your team needs to perform or execute exceptionally well on a consistent basis? Would your team answer with the same three things? If you are really brave, give your team a post-it or two and have them individually write down the answer to the above question.

_____

_____

_____

Here is an activity for a courageous leader who can truly listen with humility and empathy, who can practice self-control and genuine inquiry into another person's point of view. If you think you fit this description, then do this activity. If you honestly think you are not, then skip this one for now. For one week, ask a different person in your team each day, "How can I help you be *even more* productive at your job?" I recommend you include the words "even more" to make this a safer question to ask. At the end of the week, write a list of the responses here.

_____

_____

_____

Now, how can you deliver on the list of needs you have been given above? What will you do starting next week?

_____

_____

_____

If you assume that to a certain degree that people reflect back, in their own actions, some of the behaviors they see as acceptable by their leaders, you are kind of looking in the mirror when viewing the actions of your team. Are you happy with what you see? What are the most important three priorities or objectives supported by your team?

_____

_____

_____

What is the most important "right thing"—goal, objective, priority, project, activity that your team is not executing on to the degree needed—in terms of either speed or quality of their delivery?

_____

_____

_____

_____

What did you get done this week? What did you cross off your to-do list? Reflecting back, were these some of the most important "right things" for you to have addressed with your time?

_____

_____

_____

What is the most important "right thing" for you to do next week? Create your ten words or less headline with this answer. How will you hold yourself accountable for this action?

_____

_____

_____

But you, be strong and do not let your hands
be weak, for your work shall be rewarded!
—2 Chronicles 15:7

The main thing is to keep the
main thing a main thing.
—Stephen R. Covey

CHAPTER 5

MIRROR, MIRROR
ON THE WALL

*But let each one examine his own work,
and then he will have rejoicing in
himself alone, and not in another.*
—Galatians 6:4

*We cannot improve until we know where to
improve. Self-analysis is just like looking at the
mirror, we don't present ourselves to others till the
time we get satisfied with the image in the mirror.*
—Shahenshah Hafeez Khan

Time for a performance review! Just as feedback to your team is more effective when delivered frequently and targeted to specific actions, you giving feedback *to yourself* often is part of developing effective self-awareness. So far you have been given thirty-plus questions to process and reflect upon. That is a lot of questions! I hope that you have taken a slow and steady approach. Perhaps just one chapter every couple of weeks or so. This is not a race. You formed "you" over the years of how you have grown and matured, through the growth experiences you have had, difficult times and good times, and the mentors and influential people in your life. This evolutionary growth of you resulted in the good person you are today. However, you are an incomplete human because well, everyone is incomplete.

Furthermore, you did nothing "wrong" in how you got to where you are today. You just did not do everything right because, as incomplete humans, nobody has. So we all must keep learning and challenging ourselves to uncover our big and little flaws and then altering our own natural evolution to fill in those gaps as best we can. The ability to learn is a skill, and likely a survival skill for our careers. Peter Senge, from MIT, founder of the Society for Organizational Learning and author of the book *The Fifth Discipline: The Art and Practice of the Learning Organization,* defined learning as an enhancement of our capacity to adapt and to take actions to achieve improved performance. Key words there: "an enhancement of our capacity." So let's look in the mirror, not for the wondrous person we like to think we will see, but look for the warts and blemishes that are fixable with just a bit of intentional work on your part. You owe this enhancement in your capacity to yourself and to the people in your organization who really want you to be a great leader for their own self-interest.

You are not going to change all of that natural evolution of "you" with speed. You will grow, or further evolve you, your self-awareness, your leadership values and behaviors with a steady but *persistent* engagement in your abilities to learn. Your self-management and engagement in the *discipline* to take actions, often just small actions, to create new skills, values, and approaches to your leadership persona is where the evolution of your leadership skills comes from. Your disciplined commitment to even incremental changes and tweaks accomplished through the new actions you will take is the trigger to your growth. This disciplined commitment is not something anyone can do for you or to you. Simply put, the growth of your leadership light is all on you.

Let us begin your performance review. Look back at your answers, and especially the action items you wrote down in the first four chapters. Some things to think about at this point: Did you follow through? Did you genuinely complete the questions and especially the action items with *honesty and integrity*? I ask this because "the spirit is willing but the flesh is weak," quote from the Gospel of Matthew, or as my mother would say, "The road to hell is paved with good intentions." You need to have a thirst for learning and also a mindset to be wired to actually apply your discoveries and learnings to you leadership behaviors. To repeat a simple truism, taking the actions to grow your leadership light is all on you.

What we learn has to translate into new actions or behaviors for the learning to be effective. What have you taught yourself in the past month or several months? Are you *doing* anything different because of your answer to the previous question?

_____

_____

_____

Which set of actions were you most successful at and why do you think these were successful? Success would be defined as most impactful to evolving you to be a better leader. Therefore, you are doing something differently *and* better.

_____

_____

_____

Where were you least successful? Do you want any "do-overs"? What were the most challenging questions—and why? Where is your leadership light not as bright as you want it to be?

_____

_____

_____

How would your team answer the above questions? Have you asked them questions like these in the past few months? If you leave this section blank, this may be an area for growth in your leadership.

_____

_____

_____

Let's ramp up this topic just a bit. Where have you recently *failed*? I don't mean "failed" as in just not completing the daily crossword puzzle. I mean failed, as in something major that people knew about.

_____

_____

_____

So what did you learn? It is only a true failure if you did not examine your decision-making and become just a bit wiser at the end of the day.

_____

_____

_____

What have you learned so far about your personal style, behaviors, strengths, and weaknesses that may be hurdles and may keep you from achieving lasting growth in your leadership values, skills, and actions?

_____

_____

_____

Why will you win this challenge to grow as a leader? What is it about you that will drive you to success in your growth of your self-awareness and then growth as a leader?

_____

_____

_____

How are you defining your success? Is the success of your team and organization a primary factor in how you define your own success in your role? Or do you need to recalibrate your definition of success?

_____

_____

_____

Now the final part of this performance review. _Give yourself a grade._ You can use any scale that resonates with you. Use a letter grade of A through F, a numerical scale of 1 through 100, a 4.00 grading scale, etc. By the way, if you actually have gotten this far in the book, first of all thank you, and second of all, you at least can grade yourself at a C.

What is most important for you to do next month to grow as a leader based on your self-performance review? Create your ten words or less headline with this answer. How will you hold yourself accountable for this action?

_____

_____

_____

For if we would judge ourselves,
we would not be judged.
> —1 Corinthians 11:31

Wisdom tends to grow in proportion to
one's awareness of one's ignorance.
> —Anthony de Mello

CHAPTER 6

ALWAYS DELIVER VALUE TO OTHERS

*As each one has received a gift, minister
it to one another, as good stewards
of the manifold grace of God.*
—1 Peter 4:10

*True leadership must be for the benefit of
the followers, not to enrich the leader.*
—John C. Maxwell

The point of this chapter and the exercises is about leadership purpose of delivering value to others from your role. The "to others" is the key concept. So this is not about you and your success. This is about *being* of *value* to your team, your peers, and your organization through being of service to them. Being of service means helping others win and be successful, especially those who look to you to guide them down the path where they can accomplish something that will be valued by the organization—now and in the future. Therefore, delivering value is more than just keeping people employed and helping them with their careers or when they are struggling or dealing with problems. Delivering value with your leadership light to others is also, and to a great degree, creating meaning and an environment where people can be proud and celebrate personal and team victories.

As a leader/manager, you have several stakeholders who really want you to do great things and deliver great value—in the context of the business or purpose of the organization. If you are lucky and your organization is well aligned, those stakeholders might actually define the desired "value" outcome relatively the same as opposed to actually being in conflict with each other. Regardless, most of those desired organizational results will be rooted or directly connected to value delivered by your team. In addition, the target or definition of "great value" will change. Delivering value also encompasses guiding the team through the messiness and turbulence of change. Teams, including their leaders, will have to evolve and adopt new ways to execute their work. I doubt that is a surprise to you. You need to be the guide, perhaps even the role model, for how to adapt to the new forces and demands that the organization needs to respond to in order to be successful beyond today.

Leaders create a common goal or objective that will be meaningful and instill an atmosphere of excitement even if that goal is just for the day or the week. Don't get hung up if you are struggling to create this enchanting "vision" for the team. Oftentimes, people just need something to achieve today or this week. A five-year vision certainly looks nice on the organizational website and sounds cool to the marketplace or the customer, but your team may really appreciate a more immediate perspective from you: "What is something really good we can do this week, this month, or this year?" The long run vision is certainly important and needs to exist for an organization to have continuity and thrive, but at an individual level, in the "long run," we are all dead! So do not overlook the need to create and communicate a meaningful work environment so each week your team leaves work feeling good about themselves and how they spent a good chunk of their lives. Perhaps, substitute the word "purpose" of the team as opposed to "vision." Over the years/decades, people have become kind of numb or jaded to the flowery vision/mission statements. Purpose is defined for a team, as the reason they need to exist and do their jobs really well. Purpose can have more of a connection to a person or team's calling. A "calling," or "purpose" if you prefer, is more often an emotional or perhaps even spiritual connection to the people in a team. As a leader, perhaps restructure the organization's great vision statement into your description of the purpose for the really good things the team can deliver week in and week out. People need a purpose. People thrive when their leaders shine their leadership light on that purpose.

If only it was that easy and straightforward. Unfortunately, people, because of the way we are wired to "do things right," get good at and comfortable with delivering to a definition of success and value delivery from last month, last year, or from five years ago. Our mode of doing our jobs becomes routine and we get pretty good at it. We get kind of in "autopilot" mode. That status quo comfort level and autopilot mode then becomes organizational inertia. The term "organizational inertia" is not new and had its beginnings, perhaps not in name, in Peter Drucker's work. I like the distinction from Clark Gilbert in his article in *The Academy of Management Journal* in 2005 when he defined inertia as formed from two elements: resource rigidity and routine rigidity. The first being that organizations do not adequately invest in the management of change. The second being that people really do prefer "to do things the way we have always done them." The status quo is easy. The brain, since prehistoric man, has been wired to protect us. Protection from saber-toothed tigers back in the day has evolved to protecting our self-esteem and reputation in the jungles of today—the office. Therefore, we tell ourselves the following: *Learning new stuff and a new way is hard. Doing things that are hard will lead to mistakes and maybe failure. Mistakes can hurt and cause me to look stupid.* Stupid people generally do not get promoted. People and leaders are people too, got rewarded, thanked, smiled at, and patted on the back over time for doing things successfully—the way they have always been done. Therefore, that positive reinforcement creates an inability or lack of desire to change what got them rewarded and provided a sense of accomplishment. Positive reinforcement is a powerful conditioning agent. Organizational inertia means the fear of the "bad" often outweighs the rewards of any "good" that might come from something new. So your team, and perhaps you as well, are "playing not to lose." That is one answer to the question "Why does it take so long to get anything new done around here?" Which is a reason why effecting organizational change to achieve a new strategy or business outcome can be quite difficult. You are moving a lot of cheese (that is a reference to a good book on dealing with change: *Who Moved My Cheese?* by Spencer Johnson).

If your organization is undergoing some level of impactful change, realize the trauma that can induce. Own up to your responsibility as a leader to provide value to others and have a focus on guiding the people who look up to you through the maze (or swamp) of change. For your teams, "change" is personal. They need their leaders to help them connect and understand the change in terms of personal impact in addition to organizational impact. You deliver value when you grow the skills, abilities, and capacity of each person to handle change and make them each more valuable, now and in the future.

Delivering great value spawns the sense of pride and accomplishment in a person and in a team. "Great" value is how a leader and team take the next step to be a high-performing team that is a cornerstone for organizational success. Delivering great value to your team members and therefore the organization is part of your stewardship over the skills and talents of each person. Good people are often hard to find. Finding great people in the labor market may be close to impossible and is really a painful and costly process for you in terms of your time and the organization's resources. So the easiest route is for you to be an effective leader at developing *great* employees from the *good* employees to which you have been entrusted. It is an act of value creation when you take your time and focus your energy on making each person better and more talented to do even better things for the organization. Your own reputation in the organization will be even brighter if you are known as a leader who develops their people to the next level of their skills and builds even more abilities for them to use for the benefit of the organization. Let's now reflect just a bit on where you need to provide service and value to your team and start off with first looking to remove hurdles to their success.

You can have everything you want in life if you
just help enough people get what they want in life.
—Zig Ziglar

What is the greatest threat to the ability of the team to be successful? What slows down the team from delivering on its objectives?

_____

_____

_____

What have you done to remove or mitigate those obstacles to their success? How have you been of service to your team's success?

_____

_____

_____

What will be different about the results the team needs to accomplish a year from today? How are the objectives and measures of success visible to the team?

_____

_____

_____

The previous three reflections were at the team level. So let's get a bit more personal with some questions about the people in your team. Who has the most potential to be the top performer in the team? Who has the most potential to do great things in other areas of the organization? Who could be a senior-level leader in the organization? Who is really at the top of their game right now, and perhaps you should be looking for new opportunities for them to grow in other areas of the organization?

_____

_____

_____

Who seems to be stuck in a lower gear and not really eager to grow to get better? Who has the least confidence in themselves in the team? Meaning, you may need to do things to give some positive reinforcement. Who needs the most help to perhaps meet the bar of expectations for what the organization needs from them? Whose skills may be edging toward being obsolete in five years?

_____

_____

_____

What changes do you need to deploy that will go against the flow of the current organizational inertia and reawaken the muscles to learn, grow, and adapt in the team?

_____

_____

_____

What is the most important "*aha*" discovery for you to do next week to be of service to others in the organization? Create your ten words or less headline with this answer. How will you hold yourself accountable for this action?

_____

_____

_____

Another and broader perspective that is valuable for a leader to maintain is that your job and organization are not the center of the universe. There is a big world out there. Look for ways to offer value wherever value is needed. Use your skills to think bigger and beyond the narrow scope of your job and the limits of being a leader just during your work hours. Using your skills to help in other non-work areas is a great way to learn about applying your leadership skills and leadership light beyond the "fences" of your job. This gives you added or refined skills that will make you more effective and perhaps even open up other opportunities for you to provide value to this world. Plus it kind of might be the right thing to do—give back and be of service to others. Now "community" can be broadly defined from charitable to educational to industry associations to the local animal shelter. I encourage you to think just a bit selfishly here. Pick an avenue to help out some greater good that you will actually find meaningful and not a burden. Have it been something that you will look forward to and become energized by participating? If it advances your career or gains you some new experiences and skills, all better! Seeing new problems/issues/challenges in new teams in new organizations is a valuable source of learning. It builds your leadership and managerial toolkit and capacity to have a variety of organizational experiences.

What groups or organizations outside of your work are of most interest to you? Where can you help those groups be successful? What value can you provide them?

_____

_____

_____

Every man shall give as he is able,
according to the blessing of the LORD
your God which He has given you.
—Deuteronomy 16:17

The best way to find yourself is to lose
yourself in the service of others.
—Mahatma Gandhi

CHAPTER 7

APPRECIATE AND VALUE YOUR TEAM

And we urge you, brethren, to recognize
those who labor among you, and are over
you in the Lord and admonish you, and
to esteem them very highly in love for their
work's sake. Be at peace among yourselves.
—*1 Thessalonians 5:12–13*

The secret to success is good leadership, and
good leadership is all about making the lives
of your team members or workers better.
—Tony Dungy

The expression of appreciation and gratitude to a team by a leader is not a given cultural element in most organizations. Furthermore, the delivery of the paycheck is not same as the delivery of a genuine act of appreciation. Gratitude has to be expressed and evident in the "eye of the beholder." A key behavior that results from a personal leadership value of appreciating and valuing the team entrusted to you is that you will communicate to this team with respect in all cases. However, this chapter is not about bringing in cookies or snacks to say thanks or giving out bonuses or even walking around and saying thanks to people. This chapter will focus on an area where you communicate value and appreciation with each conversation—via the art and practice of truly listening to people. However, bringing in some cookies or doughnuts every so often is still a good thing! You certainly need to recognize and celebrate the big and little victories. Those are *key events*. But more powerful is creating the atmosphere, the culture that expresses gratitude as part of its very foundation. Honest and genuine listening with empathy and respect will communicate that you value and appreciate the person and their thoughts and ideas. You may not agree with everything, but the investment of your time and attention tells them they matter.

A theme in the previous chapters is that in most organizations, the team is usually a building block of delivering the products and services that the marketplace says has value. I will assume either you or your predecessors built the team you have today to do their work really well. I will also assume you got into your leadership and management role because you are also smart and skilled in the competencies needed by the organization to be successful. So congratulations you are a smart and skilled person. That fact can have a downside if you believe your intelligence is to the level of being superhuman, or at least (a more common situation) well above the people you are leading.

Being a "know-it-all" might not be as grand as it sounds. You certainly know a lot, but you might be kidding yourself to think you know it all. Besides truly being all-knowing and omnipotent sounds cool, but it is also quite the burden. Unfortunately, a "disease" common among those in leadership or management roles is it can cause a reversal of the neurons in the brain that gives you the impression that you are the center of the universe and your team exists to serve you. The result is that you become effectively deaf to some degree to the voice of your team. This deafness can be deadly to the brightness of your leadership light. Therefore, this chapter's exercises will examine your actions to see if you have this leadership condition of "deafness caused by excessive ego" and if so, how you can cure yourself and benefit your team and organization. I suspect Epictetus, one of the stoic philosophers, had experienced this type of ego-based deafness around two thousand years ago when he wrote, "It is impossible to learn that which one thinks one already knows."

A fool has no delight in understanding,
but in expressing his own heart.
—Proverbs 18:2

To begin, consider the reality that to some degree, the team might actually have a good deal of expertise on how the team needs to do its "thing" to contribute to the products or services the organization delivers to their customers. So listen to them. However, a common occurrence is that the title/role of "manager" seems to create the perception that they are really the true expert in whatever the team does. That might be the case, but it's a better perspective for a leader to take is that they *are not* the smartest kid in class. A really pragmatic approach to adopt is a level of *personal and intellectual humility* and treat others, especially those who just might be smarter than you, with respect and appreciation, especially for those who actually get the work done—your team.

One way a leader shows respect and honor and that they value each person is often communicated by just listening, *truly* listening, and asking for their opinions and ideas and then exploring that idea. Just a reminder here that hearing and listening are two different things. I suspect you already know that. Hearing is physical. Hearing is sound waves moving those little bones in your ears and sending vibrations to your brain in a manner that your brain has come to interpret as words. Listening is emotional or requires an emotional connection on the part of the listener. Listening is *caring* about what you are hearing. In the context of human interactions, listening at its core is an act of humility and respect with a healthy dose of empathy toward the people with whom you are interacting. This respect and humility allows you to recognize those you are listening to as having value and the ability to communicate something of value because they are smart, skilled, and engaged people.

Listening is enabled through self-awareness and self-control. Meaning, the self-control to really shut up and listen to truly understand. True understanding means we unpack the message, verbal and nonverbal (tone, facial signals, body language, etc.), factor in situational context, and then take your best empathetic shot at understanding. This level of listening is not really natural or second nature to humans. We have a million years of "survival first," i.e., fight-or-flight, burned into our brains. Therefore, great and true listening skills will set you apart from your peers and increase your effectiveness as a leader and the effectiveness and engagement of your teams. This skill will start with your conscious decision to value being a great listener then examine and practice this skill. Listening, being empathetic, having the humility to value others, effective communication, and strong self-awareness are not really just "good things" for a leader to have; they are really core skills to truly be effective in a leadership role to get great results from your organizations. These core skills are also not likely to be fads in leadership thinking. The odds are pretty good these core skills are really going to endure the test of time.

As Stephen Covey, author of *The Seven Habits of Highly Effective People*, defined "seek first to understand, then be understood" as one of the habits that become ingrained in effective people. Most people get in a habit, especially at work, of listening with the intent to solve or fix something. We listen in order to answer and display our brilliance. Or even worse, we let our *ego* drive how we listen, and our ego has a strong tendency to always want to "win" the conversation. Therefore, we do not truly listen to understand; we listen to *respond* with a decision, rebuttal, or something else to demonstrate our greatness. That approach will send pretty good signals to the speaker that their opinion and ideas are not really valued. If their opinion and ideas created from their skills and intelligence are not valued, then it is not much of a leap for people to conclude that they are not valued as people, which in turn degrades the level of engagement and passion you will get from them. At that point, all you have is a group of people who happen to be assigned to you. You have a roster but nothing close to a team.

> *He who answers a matter before he hears*
> *it, it is folly and shame to him.*
> —Proverbs 18:13

Rewind and review the last team meeting or problem-solving meeting. Did the right people speak up and contribute? Who did

71

or does most of the talking? Are your team members, some or all, reluctant to speak up? Why do you think that is?

_____

_____

_____

Would you like to have a conversation with you? What do you think people would say is your most frustrating or irritating part of your communication style?

_____

_____

_____

By the way, have you ever thought about asking someone the above question? That might take some courage and humility, but those are pretty good traits to develop as a leader, right?

> *Anxiety in the heart of man causes depression,*
> *but a good word makes it glad.*
> —Proverbs 12:25

Review the conversations of the day. Have you communicated anything positive or said "thanks"? What was the most uplifting conversation you had last week?

_____

_____

_____

Would your team know that you are glad they came to work? If so, how?

_____

_____

_____

The first part of this chapter touched on listening and realizing how much your team can offer as long as everyone is working on the same page. This section helps you examine your "style" when interacting with your team—especially when those interactions may be difficult. Also this will not be a shock to you, but when dealing with human beings, the flawed entities we all are, mistakes will be made and all sorts of difficult emotions will come into play. So this is about examining your style for the tough but often necessary aspects of your job. A key aspect to respectful communication is the time you give to the conversation. Everyone is busy. People will make assumptions of how valued and respected they are based on many things, but one will be the amount of time their manager will give them. Often that "measurement" factor is not based on hours of face time, but rather just minutes. So develop the habit and personal discipline to not "speak and run" but rather take a few minutes to just converse and interact a bit. Tell yourself to give even few minutes to ask your question, give the information or whatever, and then perhaps ensure understanding or ask for a thought or two. Just give your people a few more minutes each day to communicate you care. Also just a tip: don't look at your cell phone while you are doing this.

Time for a brief paragraph on the source of a lot of groans from probably a vast majority of managers and supervisors everywhere: the annual performance review. I have not yet come across a performance review process that generates celebrations and dancing in the halls in any organizations. However, they are important and needed to be done in some manner, and nobody really likes them. However, at the very least, the performance review is a time for a leader to show formally that they value that person. At least deliver the feedback with honesty, integrity, and have a sincere and candid conversation delivered with the purpose of recognizing the skills, contributions, and most importantly, how the person can become even more valued. Even if that conversation is about what the person *has to do better,* deliver that feedback with honesty and compassion. Those are certainly tough conversations that need to take place and hopefully did take place well before the annual review. Just think about it. Delivering the tough words of "you've got to do better" is not fun. If you did not care about the person, you probably would not be taking on the stress of this needed conversation. You would just let them eventually fail and be let go. That would seem to be the easy route. Certainly a cowardly approach.

Consider what the omission of giving any feedback, formally or informally, communicates to a person. People who never, or rarely, get feedback are really being "told" that they have no ability to change or grow or really even fit into the future of the organization. After all, why would a manager waste their time giving feedback to someone who has a low chance of actually incorporating the feedback and become a better, more valued employee? People not getting feedback will connect the dots that either they do not matter or no one thinks they can grow their skills or improve in an area.

Remember, we are all humans and therefore all flawed. Show your people you recognize we all are a "work in progress" to reaching our full potential. Show them that you value them enough to do a thoughtful and balanced job on their performance reviews. By "balance," I mean not to focus the conversation on "fixing" them. A productive part of the conversation is about how the person can leverage what they are already really good at to become even more effective for the organizations. Always or only talking about the warts will quickly become a bit disheartening for everyone. This mutual imperfection we all share heightens the need for mutual respect, genuine caring, and interdependence among leaders and their teams. The ability to forgive becomes an essential skill and habit for everyone. The performance review is a job you should perform with honesty, integrity, sincerity, and compassion.

In addition to time, respectful communication is achieved certainly by the tone and nonverbal displayed in the communication event. Tone being your voice, volume, pace, words, etc. Nonverbal aspects are your facial expressions and body language and your focus on your cell phone or computer monitor, etc. Our addiction to our cell phone screens is now a frequent nonverbal that tells the person you are talking to that whatever is displaying or might display (like a Snapchat from your kids) on your cell phone is more important than the living human being right in front of you. Therefore, you are communicating that you respect and value your electronic device more than you value a person. Bad idea. All the cookies in the world will not overcome impersonal, disrespectful, or disingenuous personal interactions with your team. Become a great and genuine listener.

What was the most difficult interaction you had recently? Why was it difficult? Did you communicate from a spirit of respect for the other person?

Was there anything left unsaid because it would have been difficult to communicate? Was there anything left unsaid that would have lifted someone's spirit and communicated how valued they are?

Did you demonstrate the value of forgiveness and that you and your team are all just human and will likely have made mistakes during the week?

_____

_____

_____

Our words are a powerful tool—spoken and unspoken. What words would you have liked to have taken back the moment they left your mouth? What damage did they inflict? Why did you want to take them back?

_____

_____

_____

Here's a quick exercise in your degree of honesty to yourself. How did your ego and your need to protect your ego and self-image impact the actions and events you wrote about in the above questions?

_____

_____

_____

_____

What is most important for you to do next week to show you value and appreciate your team? Create your ten words or less head-line with this answer. How will you hold yourself accountable for this action?

_____

_____

_____

> *Therefore encourage one another and build*
> *one another up, just as you are doing.*
> —1 Thessalonians 5:11

> *The role of a creative leader is not to have all*
> *the ideas; it's to create a culture where everyone*
> *can have ideas and feel that they're valued.*
> —Sir Kenneth Robinson

CHAPTER 8

UNLOCK THE POTENTIAL OF YOUR TEAM

*As iron sharpens iron, so a man sharpens
the countenance of his friend.*
—Proverbs 27:17

*The task of the leader is to get his people from
where they are to where they have not been.*
—Henry Kissinger

Hopefully by now you have defined the results you need from the team and the purpose and value they need to deliver. You have shown your team you want them to succeed and that you appreciate and value them. The next step is to just get out of their way. This chapter is about how to empower others to take responsibility for their team's success as well as the success of others. You want your team to be able to work fairly independent of you. If they look to you for every action or decision, then you do not have a team. You have a group of people operating like machines waiting for you to push the right buttons and flip every switch. While that may be a great ego trip, it is not a wise choice to propagate that type of culture (i.e., atmosphere) if you really want to be viewed as an effective leader. This is about giving your team a leadership light of their own to shine in the organization. In the grand scheme of things, you are just one person. The world will still revolve without you. Your organization will adjust and move forward without you. You are not the center of the universe. The sun will rise in the east whether you are here or not. Part of your legacy should be to create and perpetuate greatness in others rather than yourself. Because, and I hate to break it to you, in the big picture, you are not the end-all be-all for your organization. Just a reality check that leaders need to ponder every so often.

Chapters 3 and 4 covered having a results-focus and also having a focus on the right priorities and purpose for the team. People form into teams and then need to define a positive purpose, greater than themselves, so the team can see a reason to care—related to Maslow's hierarchy of needs. People will be open and eager to be empowered when they see and believe in a desirable future to be achieved. People want a purpose to strive toward, to accomplish something meaningful, and to be proud of. This is especially true, to generalize, with the millennial generation. That generation that will make up the majority of the workforce as the baby boomers retire out have a drive to make an impact in their jobs and careers. They want their time and talents that they are investing to matter and have value. They are hungry to work within a highly social and positive environment with a team that can truly matter and have impact to the success of the organizations. As a leader, it will be wise to engage that level of passion and commitment by giving them the skills and abilities, and then the trust, to work as highly empowered teams.

Connect the purpose of the team to an organizational purpose and value. However, it is key for you to determine the readiness or health of the organization and/or team for being able to accept increasing empowerment. Readiness for the growth that empowerment generates might be based on where the team is relative to the hierarchy of needs and the degree of trust you have generated. I will go out on a limb, but I am really just playing the odds here with this statement: your team is underutilized to some degree. In addition, the degree of "underutilization" would be the fault of their leader. That would be you. The readiness of a team to be open to the greater leverage of their knowledge and skills is influenced by two key factors in the organizational culture. One factor being how the organization reacts to negative events and the other is the chain of command for making decisions. Another "gotcha" that is detrimental to creating an empowered environment is the unwritten rules and guidelines in an organization. This was an activity for you in chapter 4—to ponder and give visibility to the invisible force in an organization that affects the ability to choose the right priorities. An undercurrent of unwritten rules, policies, values, and quirks of the management tier are often like landmines that people are cautiously looking to avoid. These landmines, and every organization has them to some degree, will effectively kill any attempt to grow empowered teams of engaged people. This is because the risk and negative result of tripping a landmine even with great intention of doing something great is not worth the reward. Also, it is foolish to ignore the landmines in the hope the team will get lucky or be wise enough to avoid them. Even the threat of these "gotchas" is enough to have people not want to step out and take a chance. Most people have heard or seen the results of tripping the landmine, and Pavlov's concept of negative reinforcement kicks in. Your team may likely think it is safer just to keep their heads down and do just what it takes to get by.

Chapter 2 spoke a bit about the idea of safety within an organization, and I use Maslow's hierarchy of needs as the definition and context on cultural safety. Another and perhaps more blunt view of this aspect of culture comes from one of the foundational thought leaders on the topic of cultural influence on motivation: Frederick Herzberg. In his two-factor theory (look it up if you have not heard about it), he examined cultural factors and defined "hygiene factors" that are essentially foundational needs to any culture to keep and attract members, especially the talent needed for the organization to survive. The degree that employees feel emotionally/psychologically safe from the actions of their managers is really the "price of entry" for any organization to provide. Without the element of safety from a punitive management culture, an organization will eventually be doomed to failure or mediocrity.

Your role in unleashing the potential of your team will probably center on the competency of the team as a whole in the practice of critical thinking in the areas of concern and influence of the team. As way of a quick definition, critical thinking is the skill to assimilate the factors relevant to a situation and determine possible solutions and courses of actions. Then analyze those options for the positives and negatives and probability of the most optimal possible outcome and then make a good decision. Therefore, critical thinking is a synergy of experience, rational thinking, holistic perspectives, and sound pragmatic judgment. As on the previous topic on motivation, critical thinking has a great deal of research on the subskills and attributes that help a person be competent at critical thinking. Odds are that the better the team is at critical thinking, the more natural or ready for increased empowerment they will be. You probably have some of the skills listed above. After all, you are reading this book, so that speaks well for your sound pragmatic judgment!

However, you may need to help your team grow as a team in this skill. Your objective as a leader is to teach and guide your team on how to discover options, make choices, and *then make the right decision*. Some simple mentoring is needed in the form of explaining how you or your manager came to make a recent decision. Explain the factors, criteria, values, and perspectives you used to guide the actions taken. That can illustrate the right way to view and think about an issue in order to help them develop the right analysis and decision-making skills, which is basically an expansion of the critical thinking capability. I suspect your decision-making is probably what you consider your secret sauce behind your success. However, as a leader who operates in the spirit of honesty, is people-focused, and driving for results for the good of the enterprise, guide your team to grow their ability to make smart decisions on a routine basis and also own the decisions they make.

Effective communication is one of the key skills and competencies that I want this book to reinforce and help you grow in as a leader. However, this is not a skill that is limited to those in leadership or management roles. In addition to the critical thinking skills, an empowered team will need to be able to have effective dialogue within the team. This means team members may need to be coached in genuine listening and respectful and *synergetic* conversations. When the barriers are down, information flows, everyone matters, and everyone contributes to the best of their ability to the problem or topic at hand. Essentially a leader who can create the conditions and the environment described in that previous sentence has moved beyond just having an effective team. That leader has created a true community of highly engaged members who will have a connection to each other that is deeper than just "teammate." This is the type of environment referred to in chapter 3 as a higher level of employee motivation within Maslow's hierarchy of needs and Alderfer's ERG model that a sense of community is one of the basic needs of a human being.

So it is not enough just to build a team of really smart, experienced, high performers. High-performing teams become even better when they evolve to consider themselves a *community* with a common sense of purpose and *interdependence*. A critical success factor will be for all those smart people to know how to work together as a team to elevate the overall quality of the team's actions. Below is some content for how a leader's actions can be toxic to creating an empowered team. However, a really smart team member who refuses to consider the perspective and contributions of others is also toxic to building an effective team. Therefore, that would be a behavior you as the leader needs to watch for and fix.

Creating empowered teams gives the team a voice that matters. People having a voice in the success of their teams and the greater organization is a foundational attribute of true and lasting employee loyalty and engagement. A premise throughout this book is that people without a voice will have low loyalty to the organization. People with low loyalty will find greener grass somewhere else and will leave. In today's job market, smart people may have more options. However, people can also just emotionally and mentally "leave" or quit the organization. They show up physically and get their work done but are pretty much just meeting the minimum. Their apathy will have turned off their creativity, passion, and caring for really doing a great job. They essentially have "retired in place." Give your employees a voice by asking for opinions, thoughts, and ideas, hopefully on stuff that matters and impacts how the team delivers value. Now, *asking* and *using* are two vastly different things. You need to create the maturity in the team that feedback and ideas are truly valued and welcome but may not always or ever be used. A voice is not always a vote. Most organizations are not intended to be democracies. Effective leaders take in and appreciate lots of good thoughts. They ponder and then select a course of action based on those thoughts or not. And, if not, take the next step of an honest leader and communicate. Why not. That is the nature of effective and empowering leadership decision-making.

I opened this chapter by mentioning the need to appreciate your team. Chapter 7 spent more time on a leadership behavior that exhibits gratitude for the people that look to you for guidance and direction. I will close out with this need and requirement for leaders to express appreciation to all those who help create success and value for the organization. Empowerment is about growth and fostering it and a leadership capacity in a group of people to become even better as a cohesive unit. This growth, founded in trust and then empowerment, generates capacity and versatility, which enables adaptability which is critical for an organization's long-term success.

Growth within a group of people in an organizational context is rarely without pain, risk, mistakes, and learning. Often the act of empowering increases their personal exposure to the consequences of mistakes. Humans stress out at the thought of being seen as someone who makes mistakes. It's part of our survival instinct. So when risk goes up, so must the upside of being successful at the job. Empowered teams are taking on more risk. A leadership value needs to be that you are more active at recognizing the wins generated by the team. Success can be fleeting. Recognize in a manner that has meaning to the team when they come through, when they have evolved from individuals to a single-minded unit with unity of focus and engagement in their purpose. Make sure your personal and organizational reward system generates tangible appreciation for the achievements of the team.

It is okay not to be omnipotent and actually admit that to yourself—every day—to not always have all the answers or always be right because we are all human and therefore flawed. This is where the people you have hired and led come factor in. Encourage them to have a voice by being open that you may not know everything all the time.

> *The most successful company is not the one with the*
> *most brains, but the most brains acting in concert.*
> —Peter Drucker

Who did you include in the decisions you made this week? Who did you exclude? And why?

_____

_____

_____

Do you think you have a community or a team? Nothing wrong with having a team, but creating a community takes that interdependence and accountability to another level.

_____

_____

_____

> *The function of leadership is to produce*
> *more leaders, not more followers.*
> —Ralph Nader

Unless you have some of Superman's DNA, your career has an expiration date. Do you have a protégé or someone you are actively coaching/developing to step into your shoes? If the answer is no, why not? How will you be accountable to yourself to be able to answer in the affirmative in six months? If the answer is yes, nice job! Give yourself a pat on the back. Now write down why you selected this person. Check to see if those reasons align the *future* needs of the organization.

_____

_____

_____

Reflect back on the quality of the conversation that took place at the last team meeting. Who did most of the talking? I talked above that empowered teams feel they have a voice. As a team, does your team really talk to a good degree? Do they pose questions to the group? Would you label your team overall as "kind of quiet"?

_____

_____

_____

Who did I ask for advice today or this week? Whose judgment and advice do you trust and whose do you not? What is causing that difference? Why do you trust them and perhaps not others?

_____

_____

_____

The greatest leader is not necessarily the one
who does the greatest things. He is the one
that gets the people to do the greatest things.
—Ronald Reagan

Track the decisions you made during the course of a week. Are you really the right person to make that decision? Are you missing an opportunity to elevate the leadership skills of others? Empowerment is a development activity. Who did you choose to let be in charge of something this week that helped grow their skills?

_____

_____

_____

Let's now look at this topic of empowerment from a different angle. The reflection exercises above focus on helping you see what you can do to foster a higher level of empowerment in your organization. But it is perhaps more important to reflect on your actions and behaviors that decrease empowerment. This chapter also presented a bit about empowerment killers. Empowerment can be a fragile concept until it takes hold and becomes part of the organization and team atmosphere and culture. Just as the organizational leader is a key influence in generating and perpetuating great levels of empowerment, most often the leader is also the primary assassin of empowerment. Your actions, words, groans, and eye-rolling are all the bullets you use to wound and ultimately kill the spirit of empowerment.

It is true that the people you are empowering are also, like you, flawed and imperfect and incomplete humans, so mistakes will be made. You and your team can do a great job at executing a well thought-out course of action, and fate will still deal you a slap upside the head. That's life sometimes. A trait of an enlightened and great leader is how they react to those inevitable mistakes. It is okay to be disappointed and frustrated with mistakes or falling short as that is what being honest is all about. It is okay to want to determine why things did not turn out as desired in order to make the people or the process a little bit better. However, often it is a fine line between honest frustration and outward anger or blaming, which leads to actions that are toxic to a person or team who are merely as human as you are and who screwed up.

Mistakes have to be acknowledged. Otherwise, you are not being honest, and you are not truly communicating the need for the team to produce quality results for the organization. To borrow a quote from General Colin Powell, "Bad news isn't wine. It doesn't improve with age." So mistakes, problems, and falling short on expected results are all "bad news"—in varying degrees. However, how you handle these issues can have a magnifying impact on the culture and psyche of the team. Ignoring them communicates that whatever happened was no big deal, so no need to improve. The "bar" on expected results just got lowered. Congratulations, you just increased the empowerment of the team to produce mediocre results! Not a recipe for long-term success for them or you. Throwing a hissy fit for every mistake or piece of less-than-desired news or results may certainly communicate the importance of getting high-quality results. However, if facing your wrath is going to be a pattern or consequence of the team trying to do right, but perhaps missing the target, then the team will no longer be eager to step up to the plate and attempt to do great things for the organization. Emotional intelligence, as part of self-awareness, creates the ability for a leader to understand what their triggers are for their own negative reactions that result in the hissy fit mentioned above.

You are not training your new puppy to not piddle on the carpet (unless of course your employees are not yet house-broken). You are dealing with skilled and intelligent humans that the organization hired to bring their skills for the benefit of the organization. So be honest, mature, positive, empathetic, and candid to bring to light mistakes in a positive manner to determine how they can improve to be smarter next time. However, still communicate that you value them and their skills. Your team, actually every team, is a unique entity or organism in the organization that is part of the organizational jigsaw puzzle that forms the "whole" of the organization to provide value to someone. As your team grows in technical skills, leadership capacity, and ability to deliver, so does the entire organization. As your team becomes less empowered and trusts less, is less engaged, less passionate, shows less initiative (most likely because of your influence), the entire organization loses energy, passion, and initiative. In short, the organization loses the ability to lead itself.

How did you react to the last negative event that took place in your team? How do you think your reaction was perceived? Did it likely erode team confidence and therefore, empowerment? Did it erode your trust in the team and therefore their level of true empowerment?

_____

_____

_____

What was it that triggered my reaction during that event? What are the top five things that will most predictably set me off down a path of negativity?

_____

_____

_____

How did you react to the last negative thing that took place in your team? Yes, I know I just asked this question. But review it from the perspective of your team. How do you think your reaction was perceived? Did it erode the team's trust in you and therefore their level of true empowerment? Answer yes or no first. Then tell yourself why you answered that way.

_____

_____

_____

Over the past month, have you given more praise or more criticism to your teams? Are you happy with the balance of praise to criticism your actions have created?

_____

_____

_____

What landmines have you buried in your organization? Meaning, what are the unwritten policies, values, and rules you have created? If you say you have none, think again—harder. If you cannot come up with any, ask the team member you trust the most to what actions will trigger a negative reaction from you.

_____

_____

_____

What is the most important habit for you to create to increase the empowerment of your team to do great work? Create your ten words or less headline with this answer. How will you hold yourself accountable for this action?

_____

_____

_____

_____

GARY HASSENSTAB

And the LORD *said, "Indeed the people are one
and they all have one language, and this is
what they begin to do; now nothing that they
propose to do will be withheld from them."*
　　　　　　　　　　　　　　　—Genesis 11:6

*Growing other leaders from the ranks isn't just
the duty of the leader, it's an obligation.*
　　　　　　　　　　　　　　　—Warren Bennis

CHAPTER 9

UNLOCK YOUR POTENTIAL

A wise man will hear and increase learning, and
a man of understanding will attain wise counsel.
—Proverbs 1:5

Live as if you were to die tomorrow.
Learn as if you were to live forever.
—Mahatma Gandhi

Finally, a chapter that is all about you! No one should be more inter-
ested or engaged in your development and growth than you. You
need this perspective of personal growth because, as I have mentioned throughout the previous chapters, you are flawed just like
everyone else. Now, there are a couple different levels of "flaws." The
most common flaw is just part of being an *incomplete* leader as every
leader is: incomplete. There are also flaws that are the signs of varying degrees of *competence*. You do need to examine your learnings
from the previous exercises holistically and see what indicates that
you are incomplete in some areas of effective leadership skills and
behaviors. For example, maybe you learned that you let yourself get
distracted during conversations. That flaw is more along the lines of
being incomplete. Another example is that you have to direct every
action your team makes because you have little trust they will do it
right, and you are okay with that. Taken at face value, I would consider that action the behavior of an incompetent leader because your
role is to get great results from the efforts of others. However, even

that damaging behavior was learned as you evolved over the years to becoming the person you are today. Everything can be unlearned and replaced with a more effective behavior that creates empowered results-generating teams. However, it does take that level of recognition and humility (to offset your overconfidence) then a *commitment* to molding yourself to take a different approach and build up a more effective leadership behavior driven from a leadership value based on personal humility and of a desire to unlock your team's potential. It does take honesty and integrity *with yourself* to truly understand what you are good at and what you are not. You may need to dial down that overconfidence gene that grows out of proportion in most managers. Then work with your strengths to build up those areas of incompleteness or incompetence. By the way, you are both incomplete and incompetent in some areas. It is those areas that define our untapped potential.

However, you may also be somewhat incomplete in some of the technical aspects of your leadership role that you mitigate with the talent in your organization. So growing you in certain aspects of the knowledge, skills, and abilities needed for your organization to deliver the needed results may not be the best approach. In chapter 7, I touched on the attitude that sometimes leaders think they need to be omnipotent and the smartest kid in class. As many a wise leader and wise authors on leadership have stated, wise leaders supplement the limitations they have in their own skills by hiring people smarter than they are. That realization is the type of synergistic action great leaders take. Realize through self-awareness and honesty that the solution is not always growing you to be more complete but to view the organization holistically and add or grow the skills needed within the team and also fill in for some of your own gaps and flaws.

We live in a VUCA world. A volatile, uncertain, complex, and ambiguous world. The US Army War College first used the term VUCA during the Cold War to describe the undercurrent of political dealings between the East and West and the impact on military strategies. *Harvard Business Review* and *Forbes* magazine used the term VUCA recently to refer to the dynamic nature of the business environment. I think there is certainly some truth that most organizations are geared toward tactically removing the "VUCA" from their worlds and instead creating stability, repeatability, and certainty. That approach to perpetuate stability may work for a bit, but at some point leaders will need to develop their capability come to grips with the realities of the new "VUCA" environment and adapt themselves through their ability to self-assess and course-correct their own leadership attitudes and values and then their behaviors to lead the organization through change. Only then can leaders adapt and course-correct their organizations to survive and thrive in a VUCA world. As Drucker stated, "The greatest danger in times of turbulence is not the turbulence; it is to act with yesterday's logic."

Your gaps or perhaps "blind spots" may not be flaws—meaning, things "wrong" with you, but might be areas that you did not need in the past to be skilled or competent. Often you just don't know what you don't know and what you need to know. I have found that it is common that leaders who have evolved in traditional organizational hierarchies and were more tactical task managers may have blind spots when it comes to thinking more strategically. Also, as organizations have generally grown in the diversity of cultures in the workplace, leaders may have a blind spot either to the generational differences or the cultural diversity and what that might mean for providing effective leadership to the organization. A common blind spot related to the organizational inertia I mentioned earlier is that leaders can be blind to seeing how the team might be organized or even do their roles in different ways to be more effective because the culture is such a strong undercurrent controlling the flow of the organization. Or how they can leverage the skills and potential of their people in different ways to add value. Leaders can be blind to how the culture is forcing their actions as opposed to the leadership values they really want to perpetuate to guide the organization.

There is "technical learning" which is valuable because every industry and market is changing and a leader needs to stay informed of the types of environmental changes and disruptions underway. However, there is a different level of learning, a more personal level of learning that is built on self-directed growth that is based on feedback from others, directly or indirectly, based on your own inner voice honed by building your self-awareness. I hope that this book and the reflection activities will help build your self-awareness capability. This chapter is about refining the ability to build the foundation of your leadership—the values that guide your daily actions and inactions and brighten your leadership light.

You must be your toughest critic and hold yourself to a standard higher than others have for you. Continue to review your performance at the end of each day or week. Use a journal. If you are serious about growing the effectiveness of your leadership light and growing your career and the careers of others, then make the time to exercise your critical thinking for true self-examination. In addition, make the commitment to an action and *write it down* to yourself.

I also really recommend you actually read, like an actual book. I know, that's crazy, right? There are so many books from brilliant authors whose wisdoms are timeless. These books are like little gold mines you can hold in your hand (or on your tablet/phone/Kindle) just waiting for you to find the nuggets. I think you should always have a book or two in progress. Read books on your industry, on the technologies impacting your industry, on creative thinking, on leadership, on managing change, on human nature, on the generational nuances in the workplace. See the list of books and authors at the end of this chapter who are leaps and bounds better than I am on the topic of leadership.

Become a role model for being an active learner to your team, using both formal education sources and the informal avenues to continue to learn about your industry, marketspace, the technologies and factors that will be creating change and most likely disruption, and management and leadership skills. Creating that personal habit of being an active learner and perpetuating that habit to the people who look to you for guidance is one of the greatest gifts you can give yourself and your team.

Use the following guidance from Peter Drucker to guide your thinking for these reflection activities: *What should I stop, start, and continue doing to be more effective?*

What have you learned that helps you be a better leader than you were a week/month/year ago?

_____

_____

_____

Ask your team for one thing you need to learn about to be more effective at being their leader.

_____

_____

_____

Ask yourself what was the most meaningful thing (to you) you worked on last week.

_____

_____

Think back to a significant decision you made this week. What was your decision-making matrix you went through? Deconstruct the steps and thinking you went through to get to the choice you made. Write down how you would defend that decision. What were the factors that influenced you?

_____

_____

_____

It is just the norm within organizations that not everything is always rainbows and butterflies. Sometimes bad things happen, people disappoint, and we disappoint ourselves. What were the triggers behind the negative actions you took last week?

_____

_____

_____

What were the values you exhibited in the choice you made? This is about assessing your actions and words and inactions to determine how those actions are representing you.

_____

_____

_____

Are you modeling the behaviors you want to see in others? Especially in your team? I predict your answer to the first question was a "yes." Which leads me to the next very important question. Who can keep you honest in the answers to the above questions? Perhaps you could find someone you respect and trust and would give you open, honest, and candid feedback to be your mentor? *Who is the most insightful person you know?*

_____

_____

_____

What will you do differently tomorrow? How will you begin to review your own performance each day and give yourself feedback?

_____

_____

_____

> *To know oneself is to study oneself in*
> *action with another person.*
> —Bruce Lee

What leadership values, behaviors, or actions were perhaps the norm for how you operated up to this point in your career that may be detrimental or no longer an effective driver for your continued success and the success and growth of your team?

_____

_____

_____

What is the one behavior or action you will change in your workplace and with your team?

_____

_____

_____

What is the most important for you to do next week to unlock your own potential? Create your ten words or less headline with this answer. How will you hold yourself accountable for this action?

_____

_____

_____

> *Whatever your life's work is, do it well. A man*
> *should do his job so well that the living, the*
> *dead, and the unborn could do it no better.*
> —Dr. Martin Luther King

Learn from smart people. There are tens of thousands of leadership books out there by thousands of authors. I have started what I consider to be the classics, like the ten books listed below. The list of authors below are in no particular order. Anything written—books, articles, essays, etc.—by anyone in this list of authors will be worth your time:

• John Maxwell	Peter Drucker	Steven Covey
• Rosabeth Moss Kanter	Daniel Goleman	John Kotter
• James Collins	Barry Posner	James Kouzes
• Max De Pree	Marshall Goldsmith	Robert Greenleaf
• Herminia Ibarra	Margaret Wheatley	Warren Bennis

These are some of the classic leadership books that should be read if you are serious about a career as an organizational leader. There are many more, but the ones below will be a good start no matter where you are in your leadership career or what "generation" you are in. These are not just books for the "boomers."

- *Becoming a Leader* by Warren Bennis
- *Tribes* by Seth Godin
- *Good to Great* by Jim Collins
- *Emotional Intelligence* by Daniel Goleman
- *The Seven Habits of Highly Effective People* by Stephen Covey
- *The Leadership Challenge* by Kouzes and Posner
- *Leading Change* by John Kotter
- *The Effective Executive* by Peter Drucker
- *The 21 Irrefutable Laws of Leadership* by John Maxwell
- *Atomic Habits: An Easy & Proven Way to Build Good Habits & Break Bad Ones* by James Clear

> *Do you see a man who excels in his*
> *work? He will stand before kings; he will*
> *not stand before unknown men.*
> —Proverbs 22:29

> *Anyone who stops learning is old, whether*
> *at twenty or eighty. Anyone who keeps*
> *learning stays young. The greatest thing*
> *in life is to keep your mind young.*
> —Henry Ford

CHAPTER 10

KEEP A HEALTHY BALANCE OF FAMILY, HEALTH, FAITH, AND CAREER

*Beloved, I pray that you may prosper in all things
and be in health, just as your soul prospers.*
—3 John 1:2

The meaning of life is to give life meaning.
—Viktor E. Frankl

Realize your job is just what you do but not who you are. Now you certainly want and deserve to have a job and career that has meaning and gives you pride and sense of accomplishment. However, your job should not be the only or even the primary source of pride, happiness, and the legacy you want to build. That would be kind of sad when viewed from a balanced and holistic perspective. You are so much more than the person putting in the forty-plus hours each week, doing a great job and providing a comfortable life for yourself and the people who are important to you. As this little book has emphasized over and over again, we, and our lives, are in many ways a product of the choices we make and the actions we take, including where we do and do not spend our time. Our values and priorities are on display throughout the day, and not just the workday.

The emphasis in the previous chapters has been on your self-awareness in your role as a leader of others. The first part of this chapter is on your self-awareness of your leadership of you. Our time, attention, and energy are the most valuable currencies we spend in our pursuit of the life we desire to build. You can have all the money you need, but it is a static currency. Meaning, it does nothing until we take the time and energy to make decisions to spend it. In addition, time is a nonrenewable currency. We can get more cash, give more attention, and have more energy as long as we eat lots of sugary candy and drink lots of coffee (just kidding). *But each day only comes around once.* You will not get yesterday back.

There also is no guarantee of tomorrow. Truly effective leaders have that level of awareness and take care of themselves in all aspects of their lives. They have the discipline and develop the right mindset as to what is important, and then, over time, make the choices that create habits that build healthy and meaningful lives.

So the choices you need to make to achieve the balance and quality of life you want is often influenced by the daily events and routines we create for ourselves. These choices and routines can be viewed as our *spending* of time and energy (i.e., investments) we make in areas of our lives that we consider to be important. I will offer up that as the leader of "You Incorporated," you should be investing in these "products" to truly add clarity and luminesce to your life's light to others:

1. *Family, friends, and close relationships*—Truly be there with your time, attention, and energy. When you are physically there, be fully present mentally and emotionally as well. This is not an original piece of guidance here, but choose family over work. Perhaps have a goal of making someone who matters to you smile every day.

2. *Your mind*—Invest in increasing your knowledge and continuous learning. Keep your mind healthy as it is the storage locker of all the knowledge and the *control panel* for all your physical parts continuing to work as desired. Manage your learning like a project with objectives and

goals. Manage your emotions to prevent the erosion that hurtful, negative, and selfish emotions can inflict on your personal control panel and inevitably damage the important relationships in your life.

3. *Invest in your physical health*—Your body, after all, is really the transport mechanism for you and your leadership light. Also, your body is aging every day—whether you like it or not. The better you feel and the more you maintain a good physical capability will pay off in your ability to be perceived as an effective person and leader. Physical balance and well-being supplies the ability to focus on developing better behaviors and skills in other areas. It provides energy to all the other areas of your life.

4. *Faith and church*—Take the time to learn and grow and practice whatever you define as a spiritual part of your life. Your spiritual life can be a source of strength, guidance, and perspective on your role in the community of mankind in which we exist.

Here's what I think the time you invest in the four items above should lead you to reflect upon.

Where/how can you make your greatest contributions in your leadership, family, and community roles? Where do your natural strengths, skills, and interests align in life for you to have a wonderful impact to those around you?

_____

_____

_____

_____

What have you done in the past week to be successful in the areas above?

_____

_____

_____

> *The noblest question in the world*
> *is, what good may I do in it?*
> —Benjamin Franklin

Your brain is a truth-seeking mechanism evolved to help manage the complexity of the human body with efficiency to minimize the overall taxation on the physical ecosystem. In other words, it really prefers the easy way to do something, the path of least resistance. The brain likes to create various "autopilot" neural connections to create efficiency. For example, when was the last time you really had to think through the physical process to tie your shoes or discover the best way to get to work? Every action you take or don't take is a reinforcement in your brain for the type of person and/or type of leader you will become, whether or not that is your intended goal. Your actions are another brick in the road of *your* life. So is your road taking you where you want to be—in terms of your family, health, faith, career, etc.? Because your brain likes "autopilot," your actions or inactions all form our habits and disciplines, including our autopilot modes for how we perform relative to the above topics. So you can *say* you are this or that type of parent, spouse, and leader, i.e., human being. You can have any belief you want to tell yourself about yourself. However, if your actions speak differently from what you say and believe, then guess what: actions win! Furthermore, your brain will believe your actions because those are physical commands you truly directed the brain to conduct for you using your physical capabilities. Those actions over time tell the brain that is what you really want and who you really are. The brain will then begin to create those autopilot pathways that make it even easier for you to take those actions without a whole lot of thinking, like tying your shoes. Those pathways will then define the person you are no matter what/who you believe (fantasize) you are. Remember the old adage "Actions speak louder than words." I would perhaps add a corollary that actions are more truthful than words about who you really are.

Changing the evolution of yourself will take time and effort, especially in the area of becoming a more balanced person in all the important aspects of your life. Perhaps a first step might be, instead of starting something, it might to be stop doing something. Stop doing things (meaning, stupid stuff) that are hindering you from being a more effective parent, spouse, leader, or just person. What is the most inane, time wasting, relationship-damaging value, action, or habit you repeat way too often?

_____

_____

_____

Let's take a quick check using one way to set a baseline for your overall balance. In the space below, write down how you would describe yourself in thirty seconds to a TV game show host.

Hi, I'm _____

_____

_____

Now, if you are really brave, ask your significant other, close friend, or family member how they would answer the question above.

Outside of work, what accomplishment in the past year are you most proud of?

_____

_____

_____

How would you continue to grow your leadership light if you were no longer employed (and did not need to be employed)?

_____

_____

_____

An individual has not started living until he can rise above the narrow confines of his individualistic concerns to the broader concerns of all humanity.
—Dr. Martin Luther King

What would you do if you won $100 million in the lottery? How would the world, your family, and people close to you, your faith, and your overall health become better? How and where would you make a difference?

_____

_____

_____

Okay, now the odds of you winning a load of cash in the lottery are hovering right around about five decimal places to the right of zero. However, in your answer to the above question, how can you make some, even small, difference with just your time and talents?

An optional question if you have a faith or spiritual life. Are you proud of your faith life? Are you doing what you think you are called to do or put on this earth to do—to some degree anyway?

An optional question if you have a set of relationships that you define as a family. Are you happy with the balance you have with where you spend your time between work and family? Do you know how your family would answer the above question?

What is your "aha" on how well you are doing at maintaining the right and healthy balance in your life? Create your ten words or less headline with this answer. How will you hold yourself accountable for this action?

As a leader, you also need to promote work-life balance to your employees and help them maintain perspective. See beyond your team's value as just cogs in the wheel of the organizational machine. Maintain your own healthy perspective on your team. They are humans with dreams, fears, problems, priorities, values, and victories beyond the walls of their workspace. Your leadership of these humans is much more than the "management of resources," at least it should be. Your role, your leadership light, is really a *stewardship* of accountability for the career success of others so they can achieve their dreams for the life they want to create. Your influence in their lives does not end each day at the end of their work shift. How you interacted with them during the day or week influences their moods and attitudes after the workday ends. Just as a person, let alone as a leader with an elevated set of responsibilities, you do not have the right to be a drain on the positive energy and optimism that humans want to have to feel good about their circumstances in life. You do not have the right to make other people miserable. In reality, it is just the opposite. You have a responsibility to do what you can to uplift and move the needle on the happiness meter for your team.

Do you know what moves the happiness meter for each of your team members? Do you ever ask about their interests and priorities outside of work, like family, hobbies, issues, etc.?

_____

_____

List each or at least several members of people you consider to be on your team. Outside of work, what is each person most proud of? If that person retired tomorrow, what would be their primary activity during retirement?

_____

_____

What is unique about that person?

_____

_____

_____

What is a source of stress for that person?

_____

_____

_____

> *To everything there is a season, a time for every purpose under heaven: a time to be born, and a time to die; a time to plant, and a time to pluck what is planted; a time to kill, and a time to heal; a time to break down, and a time to build up; a time to weep, and a time to laugh; a time to mourn, and a time to dance; a time to cast away stones, and a time to gather stones; a time to embrace, and a time to refrain from embracing.*
> —Ecclesiastes 3:1–8

> *The best and safest thing is to keep a balance in your life, acknowledge the great powers around us and in us. If you can do that, and live that way, you are really a wise man.*
> —Euripides

CHAPTER 11

WRAP IT UP—WHAT'S NEXT?

*But let patience have its perfect work, that you
may be perfect and complete, lacking nothing.*
—James 1:4

Knowing yourself is the beginning of all wisdom.
—Aristotle

I want to bring back a couple of thoughts from the start of this book.
Remember this from page 4: "*No one should care more than you about
your development and growth of leadership skills based on positive values. No one will care more, except of course, for the team of people who
are looking to you, depending on you, hungry for you, to become a great
leader and wonderful manager who will create a great environment for
them to all succeed and do things that make them proud.*"

The effort you have or will put into these exercises in self-awareness and discovery will be in direct relation to the impact you will
experience. You will live with the results of your actions. Your actions
are an outcome of the decisions and choices you make. You reap what
you sow. The choices you make are based on your values. I encourage
you to value your growth as a leader and manager. I encourage you to
value, respect, and honor the stewardship of leadership to the people
entrusted to you in your organization.

The concepts in this book will apply in varying degrees, depending on organizational culture and environment, *and* where you are at
in your leadership journey. Your growth as a leader depends primarily

on you. You supply the desire, you supply the tasks and changes you want to implement. You supply the energy and willpower to make good on these commitments to yourself. Any obstacles you *feel* are there are supplied by you. Any obstacles that you think are outside of your control might be more a fantasy (or excuse) *you* are generating. *You own you and your actions.* YOU OWN HOW BRIGHT YOUR LEADERSHIP LIGHT WILL SHINE.

However, no one, no team, no organization, no team member is in the same place, emotionally or culturally, relative to their current state or growth needs. These "states" are not static, linear, or can only move up the hierarchy of needs. Therefore, this growth is not easy. So this is not intended to be something you do once and are done. Self-awareness is a competency that is a foundational ability to help you observe, learn, change, grow, and then repeat the learning cycle.

Self-awareness *is an ability that needs to be practiced.*

> *But this I say: He who sows sparingly*
> *will also reap sparingly, and he who sows*
> *bountifully will also reap bountifully.*
> —2 Corinthians 9:6

> *Leadership and learning are*
> *indispensable to each other.*
> —John Fitzgerald Kennedy

Now, let's repeat some of the performance review process conducted at the midpoint of this book. What is your grade at this point in the journey? Regrade yourself. Use whatever grading scale that resonated with you. By the way, if you actually have gotten this far in the book, first, a tremendous "thank you." Now you at least can grade yourself at a B+. How do you get an A around here, you ask? Ask your team and your manager if they have noticed a different and better leader coming out of you recently. Ultimately, your grade perhaps should be based in large part on the performance or "grade" of the organization that you lead and the results produced by the organization. Perhaps you want to grade yourself in part on the leaders you have created. Perhaps you want to give yourself some extra credit for the number of people you thanked in the last month or the number of people who have thanked you.

How are you better since you started reading this book?

_____

_____

_____

Now, repeat the very first reflection exercise you did in the introductory chapter. If you could only build your reputation on three values, what would those be?

1. _____

2. _____

3. _____

Did any of these three values change from the start of this journey? There is no right or wrong answer. If any foundational values changed, why?

_____

_____

_____

What have you taught yourself in the past month or several months? Are you doing anything different because of your answer to the previous question? Yes, I know this is a repeat of a previous reflection.

_____

_____

_____

Which chapter or exercise caused you the most pain or discomfort to complete? That discomfort is actually growing pains. Why was it painful or uncomfortable?

_____

_____

_____

What is most important for you to do from now on to grow as a leader based on your self-performance review? How will you hold yourself accountable for this action, i.e., to create this habit?

_____

_____

_____

How will you continue to practice and grow your self-awareness?

_____

_____

_____

What is your final headline for how you will lead and grow you from now on? Where will you post this headline so it will serve as a guide for your future growth and career?

_____

_____

_____

"To thine own self be true," says Polonius to
Hamlet in Shakespeare's Hamlet.

I like this quote, but keep in mind Polonius is not really a role model for being a values-based leader. He was not a guy you could really trust. He had ulterior motives pretty much throughout the whole play. However, I will give Shakespeare the credit for a phrase that I think when taken in the context of true and genuine self-development can direct us to be the person we truly want to be. Not just who we *say* we want to be. So you could take the quote as saying "It's all about me" or that you are the center of the universe and you are the best version of you and the heck with anyone that I might offend. You can use this quote to convince yourself of your near perfection and that others in your organization need to grow. Obviously, if you got this far in this book, and you still feel that is true, then well, this book has failed.

I take the above Shakespeare quote as a call to align our actions with our values. Be true to whom we want to grow to be, to overcome the flaws we have because we are imperfect humans, and commit to even a microlevel of self-examination that will lead to growth in our leadership potential and capabilities. To use a cliché, it is a journey. The road to becoming an effective and amazing leader for your team and your organization is a road built with many bricks. Laying one brick at a time, one better habit, one more consistent action, one more positive value now more visible to the people you lead is just fine!

I thank you for reading this book. Keep in mind that the person behind the keyboard who wrote this is a flawed human being as well. No guarantee of perfection. To compensate for my flaws, my gaps in wisdom and knowledge, I brought in the words of wisdom from over the centuries. From the King James Version of the Bible, I included quotes from twenty books of the Bible, from the very first book, Genesis, to James, one of the last books, representing a span of 1,500 years, and a time in history and in organizational life that has little resemblance to today. I used several quotes from Proverbs, a book written to provide guidance and wisdom to people in a tribal society. I believe God's words and guidance are timeless when the reader takes the time to learn and apply to the context of today's world.

People are still people. I used quotes from non-Bible sources as well to demonstrate that I think God has blessed many people over the centuries with wisdom and an amazingly bright leadership light for all generations. I gave you seventy-six quotes from twenty-seven different authors—leaders from the realms of politics, the military, industry, science, Eastern and Western philosophies, and foundations of modern management and leadership. Wisdom and a bright leadership light are trademark of success regardless of the field.

I sincerely hope this little book had meaning and value to you. The world needs brighter leadership lights. Leaders focused on the values of honesty and integrity. Leaders driven to empower the human spirit in their teams to have a passion for getting great results to help drive the success of their organizations. Leaders lighting the way for the people in their organizations to have meaningful careers as part of their journey to create meaningful lives. I encourage you to challenge yourself to grow in the values and skills needed to be the type of leader our organizations and the people in those organizations need to produce greatness.

I will close with a bit more wisdom from long ago, ancient Sanskrit in this case. Sanskrit is one of the oldest languages predominantly from India and associated with the Hindu religion. This set of "rules" has been around and used by many others in their writings and teachings. These have been labeled "Rules for Being Human." I encourage you to ponder these. The last two are a good way to summarize this effort to guide you to evolve yourself, to become the you that you want to be, to be a wonderful human being to all and a great leader to the humans that look up to you for their own growth and success.

Rules for Being Human

1. You will receive a body. Use it well.
2. You will learn lessons.
3. There are no mistakes, only lessons.
4. A lesson is repeated until it is learned.
5. Learning lessons does not end.
6. "There" is no better than "here."
7. Others are merely mirrors of you.
8. What you make of your life is up to you.
9. The answers lie inside you.

So it is now up to you to light your path and the path of others. Practice the self-reflection presented here in this book, and you will find that you also have the answers to your own growth. I wish you the best on your journey.

> *You are the light of the world. A city that is set on*
> *a hill cannot be hidden. Nor do they light a lamp*
> *and put it under a basket, but on a lampstand,*
> *and it gives light to all who are in the house. Let*
> *your light so shine before men, that they may see*
> *your good works and glorify your Father in heaven.*
> —Matthew 5:14, 16

> *Who looks outside dreams, who*
> *looks inside awakens.*
> —Carl Jung

CHAPTER 12

PERSONAL GROWTH HEADLINES—SUMMARY OF YOUR PLAN

This last section is here to help you view your discoveries more holistically at the end of your journey through this book. Your headlines might be a more effective learning tool if you can see all the things you deemed as important for each chapter in just a couple of pages. You might see some common themes on your behaviors, values, goals concerns, etc. when you review your headlines as a summarized message back to you. These are your words. Take them to heart and let them guide you to future growth and success.

My headline for "Chapter 1: Emanate Integrity and Honesty" page 14

_____

_____

My headline for "Chapter 2: Be People-Focused" page 20

_____

_____

My headline for "Chapter 3: Drive for Results" page 27

_____

_____

My headline for "Chapter 4: Do the Right Thing" page 30

_____

_____

My headline for "Chapter 5: Mirror, Mirror on the Wall" page 33

_____

_____

My headline for "Chapter 6: Always Deliver Value to Others" page 37

_____

_____

My headline for "Chapter 7: Appreciate and Value Your Team" page 43

_____

_____

My headline for "Chapter 8: Unlock the Potential of Your Team" page 51

_____

_____

My headline for "Chapter 9: Unlock Your Potential" page 56

_____

_____

My headline for "Chapter 10: Keep a Healthy Balance of Family, Health, Faith, and Career" page 61

_____

_____

My headline for "Chapter 11: Wrap It Up—What's Next?" page 64

_____

_____

Behold, I will do a new thing, now it shall spring forth; shall you not know it? I will even make a road in the wilderness and rivers in the desert.
—Isaiah 43:19

*Enthusiasm is one of the most powerful engines
of success. When you do a thing, do it with
all your might. Put your whole soul into it.
Stamp it with your own personality. Be active,
be energetic, be enthusiastic and faithful, and
you will accomplish your object. Nothing great
was ever achieved without enthusiasm.*

—Ralph Waldo Emerson

CARPE DIEM

I started this book in "normal" times. When I finished, the world was changed, perhaps forever, only time will tell. The coronavirus pandemic triggered a VUCA world in overdrive. Within just months, nearly every part of the world, likely every business or organization, was reeling from the volatility to their frame of reference to how the world operated and what they needed to do to remain viable, let alone successful. Times are certainly uncertain. Organizational structures, relationships between team members to their leaders may have changed drastically in the past few months. Complexity and the "known unknowns" have multiplied, including when, if, or what is going to be the new normal.

I felt I had to review my content with regard to the values I promoted, the exercises I included, the advice I presented to determine if they are still relevant. I am convinced they still all matter and are even more critical to become a leader who can take an organization, i.e., the *people* who are even more needing you to guide them to a place, with an atmosphere of vision, hope, energy, opportunity, and gratitude. People still want to accomplish something to be proud of. They need your guidance on how that can still happen in a world turned upside down.

I will add one new perspective for you to consider. Carpe diem—seize the day. These values are grounded in making people better, making their lives better, to help them grow and achieve. What a noble pursuit, especially in the uncertain times we are in! I believe that at some point in this life, or certainly at some point, God, or whomever you believe is the higher being, will ask what you did for those who were placed in your stewardship. I do think your leadership role was not just a roll of the dice, but part of a plan. Maybe not a plan you were even aware of or had a clue about, but something guided you to this place and role in your life. Carpe diem—seize the day and grow, learn, grow others, help them learn, make them proud of themselves, and make yourself proud of you in the process.

Read chapter 10 again. Maintain the balance. Screwy times can alter our priorities, our reactions, our stressors, and stress levels. Make a habit of doing those reflection exercises to maintain the right balance to be holistically healthy and lead yourself down the truly most rewarding paths. Seize the day. Maintain the right priorities. Keep the right perspective or as Ferris Bueller put it, "Life moves pretty fast. If you don't stop and look around once in a while, you could miss it."

> *Who of you by worrying can add*
> *a single hour to his life?*
> —Matthew 6:27

> *You can make many plans, but the*
> *Lord's purpose will prevail.*
> —Proverbs 19:21

BIBLIOGRAPHY

All Bible quotes used in the content of this book are the New King James Version®. Copyright © 1982 by Thomas Nelson.

Alderfer, Clayton P. "An empirical test of a new theory of human needs." *Organizational Behavior and Human Performance* 4(2) (1969): 142–175.

Autry, J. *For Love and Profit: The Art of Caring Leadership.* Avon Books; Reprint edition, 1992.

Bennett N., and Lemione, G. J. "What VUCA Really Means for You." Harvard Business Review, January–February 2014 issue.

Buckingham, Marcus. *First, Break All the Rules: What the World's Greatest Managers Do Differently.* New York, NY: Simon & Schuster, 1999.

Covey, Stephen R. *The 7 Habits of Highly Effective People: Restoring the Character Ethic.* New York: Free Press, 2004. Print.

Gilbert, Clark G. "Unbundling the Structure of Inertia: Resource Versus Routine Rigidity." *Academy of Management Journal,* Vol. 48, No. 5 (2005): 741–763.

Goleman, Daniel. *Emotional Intelligence: Why It Can Matter More Than IQ.* New York: Bantam Books, 1995.

Greenleaf, Robert K. *Servant Leadership: A Journey into the Nature of Legitimate Power and Greatness.* New York: Paulist Press, 1977.

Herzberg, F. *Work and the nature of man.* Cleveland: World Pub. Co., 1966.

Johnson, Spencer. *Who Moved My Cheese?: An Amazing Way to Deal with Change in Your Work and in Your Life.* New York: Putnam, 1998.

Maslow, A.H. "A Theory of Human Motivation." *In Psychological Review,* 50 (4) (1943): 430–437.

Salovey, P. and Mayer, J. D. *Emotional intelligence. Imagination, Cognition, and Personality*, 9. Sage Publishing, 1990.

Schaufeli, WB, et al. "The measurement of engagement and burn-out: a two sample confirmatory factor analytical approach." *Journal of Happiness Studies*, vol. 3, (2002): 71–92.

Taylor, FW. *The Principles of Scientific Management*. New York and London: Harper and Brothers Publishers, 1919.

ABOUT THE AUTHOR

Gary Hassenstab has been in a variety of leadership roles within technology organizations for over thirty years. He has led organizations ranging from ten to one hundred technical professionals in the banking, global IT services, engineering, pharmaceutical automation, and freight logistics industries.

In order to learn more about leadership and effective management, Gary took a time-out from formal leadership roles and spent five years in leadership development as a facilitator of leadership and management courses. In addition, Gary's role was also to analyze the results of a values and competency-based assessment tool and conduct coaching sessions with the participants. He conducted over four hundred individual assessment and coaching sessions and numerous coaching sessions with intact leadership teams. Gary was also selected to be a leadership analyst and coach for the EDS executive development program. His role was to identify the experience and skill gaps for the participants and prepare targeted coaching and feedback to accelerate their readiness to take on senior leadership roles. As leadership analyst in the executive development program, Gary conducted assessments and coaching sessions on senior managers on up to division presidents.

Gary has also been an adjunct instructor for a senior-level college course on organizational leadership at Donnelly College in Kansas City, Kansas. He was also the initial chairman of the IS/IT program advisory board at Donnelly. He has written two other books, *Old School Leadership Wisdoms* and *Dear Sis, Letters Home*, based on his dad's letters from his service in WWII.

Gary lives in Lenexa, Kansas, with Cheri, his wife of thirty-five years. They have a son, Kyle, who graduated from University of Kansas with a masters in health administration, and a daughter, Carly, who graduated from Baker University with a degree in creative writing. Carly was a valuable source of editing and writing advice during the creation of this book.